La Florida del Inca and the Struggle for Social
Equality in Colonial Spanish America

La Florida del Inca and the Struggle for Social Equality in Colonial Spanish America

JONATHAN D. STEIGMAN

THE UNIVERSITY OF ALABAMA PRESS
Tuscaloosa

Copyright © 2005
The University of Alabama Press
Tuscaloosa, Alabama 35487-0380
All rights reserved
Manufactured in the United States of America

Typeface: Minion

∞
The paper on which this book is printed meets the minimum requirements of American
National Standard for Information Science–Permanence of Paper for Printed Library Materials,
ANSI Z39.48-1984.

Library of Congress Cataloging-in-Publication Data

Steigman, Jonathan D., 1967–
    La Florida del Inca and the struggle for social equality in colonial Spanish America /
Jonathan D. Steigman.
        p.   cm.
    Includes bibliographical references and index.
    ISBN 0-8173-1483-0 (cloth : alk. paper) — ISBN 0-8173-5257-0 (pbk. : alk. paper)
    1. Vega, Garcilaso de la, 1539–1616. Florida del Inca. 2. Soto, Hernando de, ca. 1500–1542.
3. America—Discovery and exploration—Spanish—Early works to 1800. 4. America—Early
works to 1800—History and criticism. 5. Florida—History—To 1565. I. Title.
    E125.S7V44 2005
    970.01′6—dc22

                                                                            2005006880

Contents

Introduction

Among the sixteenth- and seventeenth-century Spanish chroniclers who contributed significantly to popular images about the New World was the world's
original Amerindian-Spanish (*mestizo*[1]) historian and literary writer, El Inca
Garcilaso de la Vega (1539–1616) (Castanien v). He authored several works, of
which *La Florida del Inca* (1605) stands out because of its unique Amerindian
and European perspectives on the de Soto expedition (1539–1543). Since 2005
marks the four hundredth anniversary of the publication of this important
work, it seems appropriate to take another look at *La Florida* to discover why
the book has remained relevant and the object of scholarship for four hundred
years.

El Inca was born into the original mestizo generation in Peru. He arrived
upon the scene just as the New World conquest ended. Because he was half
Spanish and half Incan, El Inca lived in two worlds, and he loved them both.
He longed to see these two worlds come together into an integrated society.
He believed the Spaniards should supervise the society, replacing the Native
American's paganism with Catholic teachings. Otherwise, he wanted the Amerindians to be allowed to live as they had always lived. His writings tell us that
throughout his life he struggled to integrate his Spanish and his Inca heri-
tages. He blended the Amerindian perspective and the Spanish perspective
into one—the mestizo perspective. As a mestizo, he was connected to the New
World natives; he was concerned particularly with changing the subhuman
status into which the Europeans had cast them.

As El Inca states in his prologue to *La Florida del Inca*, he set out to give to

---

1. El Inca states, "así nos llaman en todas las Indias Occidentales a los que somos hijos de
español y de India o de indio y española" (292) ("thus throughout the West Indies they call
us who are children of a Spaniard and an Indian woman or of an Indian and a Spanish
woman"; 134).

the world a historical accounting about the Adelantado Hernando de Soto and "caballeros españoles e indios" (254) ("heroic Spanish and Indian cavaliers"; 12) in the de Soto expedition.[2] When he began *La Florida del Inca*, he concentrated not upon literature and style but upon the Spanish experiences in the New World and upon presenting what the Native Americans had been, were, and could become. Soon his outstanding literary talents burst through and, in spite of his intentions, his work became known as a New World Spanish classic (Varner 360; Menéndez y Pelayo 76–77). His writings, written in the contemporary Renaissance style, became characterized as literary art (Varner xxxiv). *La Florida del Inca* reveals, in a general sense, emotions, struggles, and conflicts experienced by those who participated in the grandiose adventure into La Florida.

When El Inca began writing in 1585, he was the world's only mestizo writer and the only American-born writer (Castanien v; Clayton xxii). His Spanish-Inca heritage and his childhood provided him perspectives that Spanish-heritage writers could not possess, giving him a uniqueness among chroniclers that has been recognized through the centuries. Incidents and experiences in his childhood in Peru gave him characters, scenes, and language to supplement what he learned about the de Soto expedition. He knew Gonzalo Silvestre, the informant for the *Florida* narrative, in Cuzco. He knew about de Soto because de Soto joined Francisco Pizarro in the Peruvian conquest in 1531, eight years before El Inca was born.

El Inca's interest in converting the inhabitants of La Florida to Catholicism,

---

2. All quotations from *La Florida del Inca* will appear in Spanish and English. The Spanish quotations are from an edition published in 1960 as part of a collection of El Inca's works entitled *Obras completas,* edited by Carmelo Saenz de Santa María. This edition is valuable because it is the same as the original edition published in Lisbon, Portugal, in 1605. I was able to verify this by comparing the edition with a 1982 edition, edited by Sylvia-Lynn Hilton, which is a facsimile of the original. Except for an updated orthography, the texts are the same. Quotations from El Inca's other works are also from the *Obras completas.*

All English quotations from *La Florida* are from *The De Soto Chronicles,* edited by Clayton, Knight, and Moore. This two-volume set contains English translations of all four of the chronicles about the de Soto expedition, including *La Florida.* This publication is useful particularly because it is a product of an interdisciplinary approach to the translation and annotation of the accounts by Elvas, Biedma, Rangel, and El Inca. This edition allows comparisons of information contained in *La Florida* with similar information from the other three narratives. The interdisciplinary presentation of the essential points of the narratives, with the inclusion of information based upon recent scholarship, makes this edition the best choice among the English translations. All other translations are mine.

Text references to *La Florida* that do not involve quoted material are to *The De Soto Chronicles.*

establishing Spanish colonization in the area, and recording the honorable and courageous acts exhibited by Spaniards and natives inspired him to compile and record information available to him concerning what de Soto and his conquistadors experienced in La Florida. El Inca's interpretation gave the world an account that is both scholarly and accessible to lay people.

When there is a true history behind a given work, it should be known before criticism proceeds. One should be a "total" scholar in the neoclassical tradition. When the historical inaccuracies that are known to exist in El Inca's interpretations in *La Florida del Inca* are weighed against the accuracy it contains, the book's relevance to historical scholarship is obvious (Quesada 152–53; Varner 360; Clayton xxi). It provides insight into not only how but also why the indigenous people reacted as they did to the Spanish intrusion into their lives.

In *La Florida*, El Inca presents Amerindian and European ethnic and cultural representations and presents his rationale, both explicitly and implicitly, concerning his presentations. The current book is a critical inquiry into these representations and into El Inca's supporting rationale and motivations.

El Inca's *La Florida del Inca* is a beautiful composition that remains the most extensive and well-written narrative on Hernando de Soto's unfortunate expedition through Florida and other areas in southeastern North America. Scholars should include this source when studying the writing style of El Inca Garcilaso de la Vega. Quesada notes that *La Florida*, because of its literary qualities, is an excellent tool with which to study "el pensamiento, la formación intelectual, las calidades estilísticas y los alcances posteriors del Inca Garcilaso" (153) ("the thought processes, intellectual development, stylistic qualities, and literary successes of the Inca Garcilaso"). El Inca writes his historical account with a purpose—to end the European self-serving, biased reports that the Amerindians were impossibly savage and barbarous. His intention is to add to the historical record an ennobling portrayal of the Native American based upon his belief in the equality of all humanity.

1
Prelude

THE CONQUEST

Columbus's sea voyage west in 1492 to establish a new trade route to India for Spain that would avoid challenging Portugal's claims to the eastern trade route to India and his consequential accidental landing at Española gave Spain hegemony over New World explorations until the mid-sixteenth century. This colonization experience was called "the conquest" by the Spaniards. The narrative form now called the chronicle was the primary communicative tool used to record and relate conquest history and the exploits and activities of conquest participants, and those who wrote these works came to be known as chroniclers. The medieval tradition of the historical romance—idealizing individuals and their deeds—suited their purpose, and these sixteenth-century writers revived this medieval epic literary style. When El Inca wrote his chronicles about the New World, a Renaissance writing style based upon the Italian Renaissance writings had become popular in Spain. He includes both the medieval tradition and the newly acquired Spanish Renaissance style in his chronicles.

The Spanish soldiers who participated in the New World conquest created an entirely new social group in the world's population. The half-Amerindian and half-Spanish children born to these individuals and Native American women were called *mestizos*. These children had to learn to integrate their two-sided cultural heritage on their own; there was no previous mestizo generation to imitate. Mestizos were treated poorly and largely ignored in the evolving cultural social orders in the New World (Varner 46–50).

When the Spanish arrived in Peru in 1531, the twelfth Inca emperor, Huayna Capac, and his warriors ruled over the inhabitants in the vast territories that the Incas had conquered in wars over centuries. Huayna Capac knew that the Inca oral history contained an ancient prediction that strangers would one day appear and conquer the Inca empire, "a story that bears a strong resemblance to the Aztec legend of the coming of Quetzalcóatl" (Castanien 14). This analogy was not a connivance between the two civilizations. There is no trace of historical evidence that either nation had any communication with, or knowledge of, the other (Prescott 1: 8). Huayna Capac predicted that he would be the last Inca and that the old prophecy would soon become reality. He ordered his people to obey these conquerors and told them that their law would be superior to the Inca law (Castanien 12–14).

In January 1531, Francisco Pizarro, the soldier Diego de Almagro, the priest Vicente de Valverde, 180 men, and 27 horses sailed from Panama in three ships and landed on Peru's shore. Charles V, King of Spain and Holy Roman Emperor, and the Council of the Indies granted Francisco Pizarro permission to explore and conquer Peru, or New Castile (Castanien 13). Pizarro established his beachhead on the island of Puná, which was close to the Bay of Túmbez, a Peruvian seaport to the south, and shortly thereafter he was joined by reinforcements led by Hernando de Soto. The participants in the Peruvian conquest cooperated while conquering the natives, but otherwise they continuously argued about each other's opinions and actions. Pizarro and de Soto were continuously suspicious of each other. Each was afraid that the other would try to gain political advantage and become the governor and captain general of Peru and enjoy all resulting economic benefits (Castanien 18).

Just prior to the conquest, the Inca ruler Huayna Capac died. Huayna Capac left his northern kingdom to his son Atahualpa, borne by his concubine. He left his southern kingdom to his son Huáscar, borne by his sister-wife.[3] He asked the half-brothers to agree to this inheritance and to live amicably with each other. With this last act, Huayna Capac subverted the Inca laws by leaving half his kingdom to a son not born into the "pure" lineage and created the seeds of discord and division (Prescott 1: 240).

In 1532, just before the Spaniards landed in Peru, Atahualpa, coveting the southern kingdom, started a civil war and captured and imprisoned his half-

---

3. Inca emperors were allowed to marry cousins, nieces, and sisters. Only one within this group could be considered the lawful wife. Imperial law required that the lawful wife belong to the Inca (ruler) line—thus the sister-wife creation. The lawful wife was always the mother of the Inca's successor. This practice was to keep "purity" within the royal family line. The Incas (the people) were taught that Manco Capac, the original Inca, and his sister-wife were sent by their god, the sun, and were heaven-born, thus uncontaminated by anything earthly. This "purity" was to be passed on through this one heaven-born lineage. Concubinage was a standard practice among the rulers also (Prescott 1: 15, 24). See also Schwartz (34) and Castanien (90).

brother, Huáscar. His army chased his southern-kingdom kinsmen to a plain north of Cuzco, where his warriors encircled their captives and attempted to complete the genocide ordered by Atahualpa. Among these captives were two children—the Palla Chimpu and her brother Hualipa—El Inca's mother and his uncle.[4] The guards allowed children younger than eleven years old to escape. The Palla Chimpu and her brother were within this age group and were allowed to slip away to safety (Varner 12).

By this time, Francisco Pizarro and a small contingent of his army had landed at Túmbez and were proceeding toward Atahualpa's residence, Cajamarca. Atahualpa could have conquered the Spaniards rather than having the Spaniards conquer him, but apparently he believed that they were sons of Viracocha, the white-skinned and bearded god of the sun, and had come to fulfill the ancient prophecy told by Huayna Capac. Rather than confront the Spaniards, Atahualpa "retreated to his suburban baths and left . . . noblemen to render to the invaders those luxuries due men descended from the Sun" (Varner 13). When de Soto and Pizarro visited Atahualpa at his retreat, he thought the Spaniards resembled the legendary Viracocha, as well as the image that the eighth Inca had asked to be carved on a stone portraying the Viracocha apparition he said he had seen when he was a prince, banished by the seventh Inca to the sheep pastures at Chita to effect a change in his attitude (Varner 13).

The Spaniards plotted to capture Atahualpa by extending to him an invitation to meet in Cajamarca. Atahualpa accepted the invitation, and the two leaders and their armies came together on November 16, 1532—the first encounter between official representatives of these two alien civilizations (Castanien 13). When Atahualpa arrived in the town, the priest Valverde appeared before him and began explaining Catholic doctrines, which the Spaniards expected him to accept. It is unlikely that Atahualpa perfectly understood what the interpreter who had accompanied Pizarro from the coast told him. He probably did understand, however, the suggestion that he should recognize the authority of the Spanish king (Castanien 15). Atahualpa asked the priest upon what he based his authority. The priest answered by giving Atahualpa a religious book.[5]

---

4. A "Palla" was any woman who belonged to the Inca royal family. El Inca always referred to his mother with this title (Varner 388).
5. Castanien states that the book in question may have been a breviary (prayer book) (15). Patricia Galloway believes the text was the "*requerimiento*" (32). Galloway states that the *requerimiento* was the "text to be read to the Indians when offering them a spiritual good and demanding obedience" (16). Spanish law required that the *requerimiento* be read to the Native Americans. Schwartz notes, "A system had been developed by the early 1500's whereby a 'requerimiento' (requirement) was read aloud before invasion of a new area. The 'requeri-

Atahualpa glanced at the book and threw it upon the ground. Pizarro used this incident as the excuse to arrest Atahualpa. He gave the signal to attack, and his soldiers began to slaughter the natives. Within half an hour, Pizarro and his forces had killed more than three thousand Amerindians, winning a very one-sided victory (Varner 14).

Huáscar's murder was ordered by Atahualpa and executed by his loyalists after the Spaniards put Atahualpa into prison. Pizarro wished to use the murder of Huáscar as a pretext to execute Atahualpa immediately, thereby avoiding the possibility of his leading a native revolt against the conquering Spanish. De Soto believed that Atahualpa should be sent to Spain to receive a fair trial and due process of law. This desire on the part of de Soto was probably due less to a sense of justice and more to the fact that Atahualpa was more useful to him than to the Pizarros: "Soto's attitude toward Atahualpa had elements of fair-mindedness, generosity, and chivalry, but there was also another dimension . . . Atahualpa alive and free would represent a threat to the rulers of Peru, the Pizarros, but for Soto . . . such a fluid and insecure situation might bring with it great opportunities" (Lockhart 191, 196). During a period in which de Soto was absent, Pizarro and his forces put Atahualpa through a pretend trial and executed him (Varner 14–15; Castanien 15).

Not only was Atahualpa's execution by Pizarro considered extraordinary but also the way he and his army plundered and pillaged the natives' possessions was shocking. The 169 Spaniards who marched across the highlands to Caja-marca secured over a million pesos for division, with horsemen receiving some 8,800 gold pesos and 362 marks of silver and footmen about half that amount. Brading writes, also, that the Pizarro brothers sent the Spanish king 153,000 gold pesos and 5,058 marks of silver (31).

After Atahualpa's execution, Francisco Pizarro led his army to the ancient Inca capital, Cuzco, and set up a Spanish-type government. While engaged in this task, he received word that another army was arriving in Peru, led by Pedro de Alvarado, who was already known for his exploits with the Cortés army in the Aztec capital, Tenochtitlan. Alvarado believed that Pizarro's claims excluded the northern Inca kingdom, Quito. He organized an expedition, which

---

miento' stated that the Indians should submit to the temporal crown of Spain and to the spiritual head of Christianity, the Pope. When this had been read and peaceful submission was not forthcoming, then Spanish troops felt justified in conducting the cruel arts of their warfare" (79). Varner notes that interpretative inadequacies could have contributed to Atahualpa's *requerimiento* rejection: "Through the lips of an interpreter[,] . . . a despicable coastal Indian who, even had he known the language of Cuzco, would have been hard pressed to find Quechuan words to clarify Spanish ethics and mysticism, the devout religious attempted to explain his theology" (13).

included about five hundred men, to explore this region. It was this expedition that brought Captain Sebastián Garcilaso de la Vega, El Inca Garcilaso de la Vega's father, to Peru. No date for his departure from Spain is available, but historians believe that Sebastián Garcilaso de la Vega joined Alvarado's expedition in Spain in July 1528 (Castanien 15). Historical evidence corroborates that he was with the Alvarado army in Guatemala in 1531.

Castanien describes the ensuing events:

> Pizarro, whose ideas of his own rights did not correspond with those of Alvarado, sent his partner, Diego de Almagro, to challenge the intruder. By the time the two met, it was obvious that it was mutually advantageous to join forces. Alvarado had discovered that the kingdom of Quito did not offer all the rewards he had hoped for. Almagro and Pizarro could make good use of the additional strength offered by Alvarado's army. (16)

At this point, the Alvarado army, including Captain Garcilaso, joined the Pizarro army. Thus began the Pizarro-Garcilaso association that was to so greatly affect El Inca's life. The ever-threatening civil war in Peru was postponed, although this reprieve was short-lived.

In 1534, Francisco Pizarro returned to Peru after a visit to Spain and brought with him new land grants given to him by the king that allowed him and his brothers to gain economic advantage over Diego de Almagro, his partner. Feeling that his land grants were of poor quality, Almagro captured Cuzco, an act that provoked the full-scale civil war that caused such suffering in Cuzco and other areas in Peru. Francisco Pizarro and his army eventually captured and executed Almagro and stole his land grants. This provoked Almagro's allies and his mestizo son to plot vengeance against Francisco. On June 26, 1541, they entered his home in the colonial capital and killed him. Gonzalo Pizarro replaced his brother as the army's commander. The younger Almagro was captured in battle and executed, which ended this phase in the Peruvian civil war. Peace, however, was not yet to be (Varner 34–38, 46–49).

THE NEW LAWS

In Spain in the 1540s, the public was shocked and unhappy with the news about events in Peru. Charles V—the Hapsburg prince who had inherited the Spanish throne because his mother, married to a Hapsburg, was the daughter of Ferdinand and Isabella—was absorbed by interests in his European empire and had allowed Spain's New World empire to progress almost unheeded by his court (Prescott 2: 173). The land and the natives were "appropriated by the victors as the legitimate spoils of victory; and . . . outrages were perpetuated . . . at contemplation of which humanity shudders" (Prescott 2: 174).[6]

In 1541, after having been in Germany overseeing his German interests, King Charles revisited Spain, "where his attention was imperatively called to the state of the colonies" (Prescott 2: 178). No one pressed the issue as strongly as Bartolomé de las Casas, the priest called "Protector of the Indians" because his attitudes and actions toward the Amerindians were so benevolent. Las Casas had just completed his well-accepted treatise on the Spanish destruction of the Indies, and he gave his manuscript to Charles V in 1542. That year, a council was called, comprised chiefly of jurists and theologians, to write laws to govern the Spanish colonies (Prescott 2: 178). Las Casas, "the uncompromising friend of freedom" (Prescott 2: 179), appeared and presented the proposition that Amerindians were free by the law of nature and that they had a right to the Crown's protection. His arguments prevailed, and the council passed a code of ordinances called "The New Laws." The laws received the king's approval, and in 1543 they were published in Madrid. The ordinances threatened the economic security of the colonial landholders. The news "was conveyed by numerous letters to the colonists, from their friends in Spain. The tidings flew like wildfire over the land, from Mexico to Chile" (Prescott 2: 181). The laws applied to all Spain's colonies. A number of provisions had an immediate effect upon Peru. First, the laws stated that the Amerindians were true and loyal vassals of the Crown and were to be free. Yet, to keep the promises the government had given the conquerors, those who lawfully owned Indian slaves could retain them until the next generation, at which time the slaves were to become free. Second, slave owners who had neglected or ill-used their slaves would lose them. Third, slave ownership by public functionaries, ecclesiastics, and religious corporations would end. Fourth, all who had taken a criminal part in the Almagro and Pizarro feuds would lose their slaves. Fifth, Indians should be moderately taxed; they should not be compelled to labor where they did not choose and where from particular circumstances this was necessary, they should receive fair compensation. Sixth, the excessively large land grants should be reduced, and seventh, the landowners who had been notoriously abusive to their slaves should lose their estates altogether (Prescott 2: 180; Castanien 19).

Cristóbal Vaca de Castro was sent to Peru in 1541 by Charles V to work with

---

6. "[T]he manner in which the Spanish territories of the New World had been originally acquired was most unfortunate both for the conquered races and their masters. Had the provinces gained by the Spaniards been the fruit of peaceful acquisition—of barter and negotiation—or had their conquest been achieved under the immediate direction of the government, the interests of the natives would have been more carefully protected" (Prescott 2: 173–74).

Francisco Pizarro to calm the social unrest caused by the provisions of The New Laws, and he became governor upon Pizarro's death. He was unable to calm the upheaval caused by the new ordinances, so the king sent a viceroy (royal representative), Blasco Núñez de Vela, to Peru to regain governmental authority and to implement The New Laws.[7]

Núñez de Vela was unable to promulgate these laws because his approach was "high-handed" (Brading 30) and was provocative to Gonzalo Pizarro, who by this time had become a very influential landholder. The participants in the civil war between Francisco Pizarro and Almagro were in danger of losing their land grants, and "the entire land was inflamed, but the turmoil at Cuzco exceeded that of any other city" (Varner 57). In accordance with the royal decree establishing the office of viceroy, Vaca de Castro resigned upon Núñez de Vela's arrival and ceded all governmental authority to him (Varner 69).

In 1544, before stepping down, the governor had bestowed upon Captain Garcilaso five Indian towns in Havisca that had belonged to Francisco Pizarro, as a reward for his help in defeating the younger Almagro's forces in the Battle of Chupas on September 16, 1542. With this new acquisition added to his other landholdings, Captain Garcilaso qualified as one to be severely targeted by The New Laws. Captain Garcilaso was willing to join with others to choose someone to present their cause to the king's viceroy in Peru's new governmental center, Los Reyes, but he wanted to stay loyal to the Spanish government. The group thought that Gonzalo Pizarro was the logical person. The petition that they presented to him included no seditious intent or overtones. Captain Garcilaso and others "apparently had misjudged Gonzalo Pizarro, since . . . there lurked a stubborn determination which could not be satisfied with subservience to a viceroy who threatened . . . economic ruin" (Varner 57). Pizarro believed that the new viceroy would not be willing to negotiate and that the armed strength of the landholders should be employed in the pursuit of their cause.

As Gonzalo Pizarro prepared to embark upon the journey to Los Reyes, Cuzco began to look like an armed camp:

7. Bartolomé de las Casas, a Catholic bishop, who had witnessed much of the New World conquest, published a book in 1552 entitled *Brevísima relación de la destrucción de las Indias* (*Brief Account of the Destruction of the Indies*) in which he described the atrocities committed by the Spanish against the Native Americans. He recommended to the Spanish king abolition of the land grant system that put the Amerindians into de facto slavery, and he called for an end to violence against the natives. He stated his belief that the Amerindians were inherently good, rational beings and that the Spanish conquerors were greedy and not interested in the well-being of the natives (Ross 93–97). The king and his council incorporated Las Casas's ideas into The New Laws.

[M]any were alarmed lest what purported to be a peaceful and justifiable plea should eventually come to be regarded as a manifestation of sedition. Captain Garcilaso, among others, remonstrated privately with Pizarro, but the latter quickly excused the militant aspect of his preparations by referring to necessity for protection along the highroad against the guerillas of the Inca Manco and in Los Reyes against the Viceroy himself, who was known to have boasted of the power to deprive Pizarro of his head. (Varner 58)

Captain Garcilaso and others wished to comply with the viceroy's summons to Cuzco's citizens to travel to Los Reyes and submit to the king's authority; however, when Pizarro threatened to withdraw entirely, along with his well-equipped army, the other estate holders, including Captain Garcilaso, agreed to continue to support him. On the road to Los Reyes, Garcilaso and other officers who wished to remain loyalists deserted Pizarro's army. They preceded Pizarro to Los Reyes and joined the viceroy's company; however, Viceroy Núñez de Vela, not willing to confront the rebel army, had left by the time Garcilaso and company arrived, leaving the *Audiencia* as the king's only representatives in the town (Varner 56–68). A council of judges created to assist the viceroy in adjudicating land disputes and enforcing The New Laws, the *Audiencia* had no ability to field an army larger than the fifty soldiers that garrisoned Los Reyes and quickly capitulated to Pizarro when he arrived, after which he proclaimed himself governor. Captain Garcilaso went into hiding, but he eventually was captured by Pizarro's men and held in house arrest. Pizarro's forces, accompanied by Captain Garcilaso under house arrest, defeated Núñez de Vela's forces on November 19, 1546, in a battle fought near Quito (Varner 70).

Meanwhile, Charles V had dispatched another administrative emissary to Peru named Pedro de la Gasca. With the simple title of "president," he was empowered to implement The New Laws by whatever means necessary. Whereas Núñez de Vela had been reckless and had exercised poor judgment, which led to his defeat, Gasca was skillful and cunning. He was able to martial enough loyalist forces to attack Pizarro's rebel force at Huarina on October 26, 1547. Pizarro's forces, however, after a long and desperate battle, defeated Gasca's loyalist forces. Present at the Battle of Huarina, though not a direct participant, was Pizarro's prisoner, Captain Garcilaso de la Vega.

While Garcilaso was in this imprisoned status, an incident occurred that later would badly affect his son, El Inca Garcilaso de la Vega. The gossip that got recorded was that Pizarro's horse had been killed in the Huarina battle and that Captain Garcilaso turned the tide against the royalists by lending Pizarro his horse. Pizarro was able to rally his troops, as the story went, and rout the king's forces. The truth was that the battle had already ended when Pizarro gained Garcilaso's horse (a horse that, ironically, Captain Garcilaso had purchased with a loan from Pizarro). Pizarro's own horse was slightly wounded, and he did not want to enter Cuzco on a wounded horse (Varner 70–81).

Captain Garcilaso escaped to the loyalists' side just before the conclusive Battle of Sacsahuana on April 9, 1548, where Pedro de la Gasca, having recovered from his defeat at Huarina and rebuilt his forces, conquered the rebel army and beheaded Gonzalo Pizarro. With the defeat and execution of Pizarro, Gasca and his army restored to Peru the law and order that had been lost sixteen years earlier in 1532 (Varner 85–90).

EL INCA'S BIRTH AND HERITAGE

On April 12, 1539, seven years after the Spanish arrived in Peru and well into the civil war period, a son was born to Palla Chimpu Ocllo (baptized Isabel Suárez), an Inca princess, and Captain Sebastián Garcilaso de la Vega y Vargas. He was "the future historian of his mother's people and of their defeat by his father's people . . . Peru's first truly distinguished man of letters, christened with the name of his Spanish great-grandfather, [who] chose later to be known as The Inca Garcilaso de la Vega, a name with which he proudly advertised his double heritage" (Castanien 18). The baby was given the name Gómez Suárez de Figueroa.

Gómez's parents belonged to societal groups that were somewhat conspicuous in their respective cultures. Captain Sebastián Garcilaso de la Vega belonged to the Spanish noble class known as *hidalgos.* Chimpu Ocllo carried the title *palla,* which signified she belonged to Inca nobility. It was not, however, his descent from Inca nobility that gave Gómez royal status; rather, it was the Inca superstition about Viracocha. Believing the legend, the natives regarded the elder Garcilaso and his comrades as semidivine, thus imparting to their children a special status. Gómez was entitled to use the royal title "Inca" because of "his having been sired by a fair-skinned conquistador whom the Indians had superstitiously regarded as a viracocha and thus a legitimate descendant through the male lineage of the Moon and the Sun" (Varner 43).

Captain Sebastián Garcilaso de la Vega's parents, doña Blanca de Sotomayor Suárez de Figueroa and Alonso de Hinestrosa de Vargas, had nine children. Gómez's father was born in Badajóz, Extremadura, Spain, sometime between 1500 and 1510. He grew up in Badajóz and received a gentleman's education, which included horsemanship and arms. In those days, Spanish custom required that young men with noble inheritance be employed by the king's court or the army or that they enter the priesthood. Among his maternal relatives were some well-known Spanish writers. His mother was related to prominent figures in medieval literature, such as Pedro Lopez de Ayala and Fernán Pérez de Guzmán. The most prominent of doña Blanca's relations was her soldier-poet cousin Garcilaso de la Vega, who helped to revive Spanish poetry in the sixteenth century through his innovative use of Italianate meters. Military accomplishments characterized Gómez's paternal ancestral lineage. One ancestor, García Pérez de Vargas, assisted Fernando I in his battle with the Moors in Andalucía during the reconquest of the Iberian Peninsula. In Peru, Captain Sebastián Garcilaso de la Vega was accepted into the ruling class and was rewarded with estates, slave Indians, and the royal administrative office of *corregidor* of Cuzco.

Chimpu Ocllo was the granddaughter of the eleventh Inca emperor, Tupac Inca Yupanqui, the niece of the legendary twelfth Inca emperor Huayna Capac, and the cousin of the famous Atahualpa and the lesser-known Huáscar. She was the daughter of Huallpa Tupac Inca Yupanqui, who was the younger brother of Huayna Capac. Since she belonged to the family of Huáscar, the loser in the civil war that preceded the arrival of the Spanish, she and her brother very narrowly escaped death at the hands of Atahualpa's victorious forces. Her perspective was unique, as she was a witness to both the war of Inca succession and the Spanish conquest of her native land. Having heard the ancient prophecies, she, too, believed the Spanish were descendants of Viracocha. Unable to marry her common-law husband, Captain Garcilaso, she married a Spanish colonist of a lower economic status and adopted a Spanish name. El Inca Garcilaso, in his dedication to *Diálogos del amor* (*Dialogues of Love*) (1590), refers to her as "la Palla doña Isabel" (11). She never learned to read or write Spanish. On November 22, 1571, she dictated her will to an interpreter, and it was signed by a witness because she "did not know how to sign her name" (qtd. in Castanien 21).

EL INCA'S CHILDHOOD

Gómez's childhood and adolescent years were spent in his birthplace, Cuzco. This ancient town was built and named by the Incas when they established their empire.[8] The Spanish later superimposed upon Cuzco their lifestyle, gov-

8. With regard to the founding of Cuzco, it is impossible to determine an absolute date for this event, since the Incas had no written language with which to record their history and did not think of time in the same way as Europeans thought about it. When talking about the past, the Incas considered something that happened ten years prior to be no more recent than something that happened a thousand years prior; all that mattered to them were the events of history, not the times in which they occurred. According to Bernabé Cobo, a priest who spent years living among the Incas during the colonial period, they did not even keep track of the ages of individuals. The closest archaeologists can come to a date for the founding of Cuzco is approximately A.D. 1100 (Schwartz 36–37).

ernment, and culture. When Gómez was born in Cuzco in 1539, the civil war between conquistador groups in Peru had been going on for seven years. This conflict kept the society in turmoil until he was nine years old. Years later, Gómez wrote about this time in his life:

> En mis niñezes oy una poca de gramática, mal enseñada por siete precep-tores que a temporadas tuvimos, y peor aprendida por pocos más discí-pulos que éramos, por la revolución de las guerras que en la patria avía, que ayudavam a la inquietud de los maestros.[9]

> In my childhood I learned a little grammar, poorly taught by seven in-structors that we had at various times, and worse learned by we few stu-dents, because of the turmoil caused by the wars that were going on in the land, and which added to the uneasiness of the instructors.

Captain Sebastián Garcilaso de la Vega legally acknowledged Gómez as his son. Such acceptance by his Spanish father gave him some advantages over oth-ers in this original mestizo generation in Peru. For example, his Spanish-Inca heritage resulted in a two-part education. He received a European-style pre-paratory education from Juan del Cuellar. A priest who lived in Cuzco, Cuellar tutored Gómez and several other mestizo students and taught them Spanish and other subjects that were considered to be important to the Spanish educa-tion system at that time. Cuellar aspired to send all his students to the Univer-sity of Salamanca, although Gómez never went. Such thinking shows that, un-like other priests in that time and place, he did not assume that the Incas were intellectually inferior to Europeans. Gómez learned Inca oral history (the Incas had no written language), traditions, and mythology from his mother and her relatives, primarily his uncle. This oral history included his family's hereditary role in the Inca hierarchy. When he was young, he listened to tales about his mother's ancestors, told to him in the Inca language, Quechua. He learned Quechua and the Incas' *quipu,* a mnemonic system involving knots placed into cords, with which the Incas kept statistical records and sent messages by relay runners throughout the empire. In his teenage years, he studied Spanish and Latin with another tutor, Juan de Alcobaza. Gómez was 13 or 14 years old when his tutelage by his Spanish instructors ended.

Gómez's parents lived together for several years in the large, tile-roofed, Spanish colonial house the captain owned in Cuzco, though they never married each other. Neither the society nor the Catholic Church spoke against this

---

9. This quote is from a letter that El Inca wrote to a fellow scholar, Juan Fernández Franco, in late December 1592. The letter appears in unexpurgated form in Asensio.

practice. Some historians claim that Spanish soldiers who had attained rank were allowed by the Spanish government to live with Indian women, but they were not allowed by law to marry their Indian companions nor to claim their mestizo children legitimately. However, *The Cambridge History of Latin America* states, "the crown's initial policy of encouraging marriages with indigenous women was abandoned by the mid-sixteenth century, and replaced increasingly by an official policy of separation and protection of the Indians. Intermarriage was never barred; it apparently lost personal appeal and social prestige" (MacLeod 348). Captain Garcilaso abandoned Gómez's mother and married a Spanish aristocrat, Luisa Martel de los Ríos, in 1551, and shortly thereafter, Isabel married a working-class Spaniard. After these marriages, the teenager lived with his father as long as Captain Garcilaso lived.

Cuzco was a busy and bustling crossroads community. Even with civil war raging at that time, Cuzco was considered a Spanish cultural center. Captain Garcilaso de la Vega often entertained other Spaniards in his home, particularly including his comrades from the armies that had conquered Peru during the original Spanish *entrada* (invasion). During this time, Gómez became acquainted with Gonzalo Silvestre, who had accompanied de Soto to Florida. Years later, having returned to Spain and reacquainted himself with Gómez (who had changed his name to Garcilaso de la Vega), Silvestre related to him the experiences that became *La Florida del Inca*. It was at his father's table that Gómez also became acquainted with Gonzalo Pizarro after he had assumed the leadership role left vacant when his brother Francisco was killed. In this role he resided in Cuzco, and Gómez played with Pizarro's mestizo son. Gómez also visited in the Pizarro home and, after the Huarina battle, sat next to Pizarro at the dinner table as he and his comrades celebrated their victory. Pizarro gave the young boy food from his own plate. Gómez came to appreciate and admire this Pizarro brother:

> Pizarro . . . took pleasure in his own half-caste offspring as well as in those of his brother . . . He was attracted by Captain Garcilaso's *mestizo,* treating the lad as if he were his own son. Thus Gómez became a companion of Fernando and Francisco Pizarro, the rebel's son and his nephew, and through this association he often was brought into the presence of the genial commander . . . These whispering *conquistadores* had no way of knowing that they were etching their biographies in the pliant mind of a little half-caste boy. And yet Gómez in after years remembered Gonzalo Pizarro, not as the tyrant, thief, and adulterer that some said he was, not as his father's oppressor, but as a great, handsome, and gentle person, a magnificent horseman in both the Moorish and the Spanish saddles, who rode about the streets of Cuzco in fine toggery, receiving the homage of

all manner of people, doffing his hat to each and every one, and addressing them as "Your Grace." (Varner 84–85)

Gómez suffered in Cuzco society, in part because his mestizo group was
marginalized and because the civil war kept the society on edge. He was also
troubled by his parents' never having been married. Perhaps the worst pain
suffered was caused by the well-intentioned but very abusive New Laws. Stipu-
lations in these laws had tragic consequences upon his life. Not only were they
hurting his Amerindian relatives by ending the paternal relationship between
them and the Spaniards, but they also probably contributed to his parents'
separation. Men were required to be married to receive consideration when
land was reassigned under the new ordinances.

Although his residency in Cuzco was brief, what he learned and experienced
there became a cornerstone of his writings. The Inca oral history, traditions,
and mythology told to him by his mother and her relatives in this time held
sway in his writings and inspired him to write what is today considered his best
literary creation, the *Comentarios reales de los Incas* (*Royal Commentaries of
the Incas*) (1609). The relationship with Gonzalo Pizarro became verbalized in
the *Historia general del Perú* (*General History of Peru*) (1617). The acquaintance with Gonzalo Silvestre gave Gómez (Garcilaso de la Vega, El Inca) his *La
Florida del Inca.*

GÓMEZ GOES TO SPAIN

In 1559, a long illness eventually killed Captain Sebastián Garcilaso de la Vega.
Gómez immediately initiated plans to travel to Spain, which "some say . . . had
been instigated by don Sebastián himself . . . and others have suggested . . . was
an idea of Philip II who was beginning to fear the rising influence of this young
mestizo among the Children of the Sun," as the Inca people referred to themselves (Varner xxvii). Other historians suggest that he wanted to seek his inheritance, the land grants in Peru that had been awarded to his soldier parent.
Captain Garcilaso, in his will, provided an income in Spain to support his son
when he arrived:

[O]n January 18, 1560, Antonio de Quiñones, securing transcripts of Captain Garcilaso's will, empowered Ruy López de Torres and Alexis González
Gallego, merchants of Cuzco and Los Reyes respectively, to transfer four
thousand pesos in silver bars to Francisco de Torres, brother of Ruy
López, at Seville, where they were to be held for collection by the Captain's brothers. This apparently was to be the *mestizo*'s sole source of income in Spain. (Varner 189)

On January 20, 1560, Gómez departed from Cuzco, the only place he had ever lived in his short twenty years. He left his mother and all the acquaintances he had ever known, with the exception of the two companions who accompanied him, one traveling with him to Los Reyes and the other continuing to Spain. He was embarking upon a long trip to a country and a society to which he had been given a verbal introduction but had never known. He and his two companions set out on the trail leading to Los Reyes and the sea. Los Reyes was ten or twelve days' travel, one hundred and twenty leagues, through mountain passes, through the Andean peaks and the sierra high desert, where, at night, strong winds blew and the temperatures went to below freezing. Shelter was difficult to find because "[t]here were no *tambos,* or inns, and travelers along that desolate route either sought shelter from natives or friends or, in the icy regions, huddled hopefully together in the darkness, both man and beast, to draw what life-giving warmth they could from each other" (Varner 191–92).

The mountain passes were crowded with pack trains carrying ore to the ships at the Port of Callao. Before reaching the Andean crest, Gómez passed through areas and battlefields where Captain Garcilaso had participated in battles years earlier. After crossing the hazardous Andes, the travelers experienced the scorching coastal sands with insect populations that bit and stung. Traveling north through the *pampa* to the Hinarro Valley, he was able to visit with a gentleman who had been a servant to Captain Garcilaso. When he arrived in Los Reyes shortly thereafter, Gómez was hounded by gnats. Though houses in Los Reyes had screens, the screens gave incomplete protection. People had begun to refer to Los Reyes as Lima, a perversion of *Rimac,* which was the Quechua name that had been given to the nearby river. Varner provides a vivid word-picture about Gómez's experiences in Lima:

> Yet as he now approached, anticipating colorful towers and battlements, he beheld only flat dwellings with mud roofs typical of Spanish coastal architecture. Houses were commodious and situated on streets of great breadth with encompassing tropical gardens, but enveloped in heat—heat that . . . brought a stench from the iron head cages in the plaza where still could be seen . . . visages of bold men he once had known well in Cuzco[,] Francisco de Carvajal, Gonzalo Pizarro and [. . .] Francisco Hernández Girón. . . . All about him lay poignant reminders of his father's perilous days at Los Reyes. (193)

Varner states that, in February, Gómez boarded a ship at Callao and started his hazardous trip through Panama to Spain (198). This journey, along with Gómez's experiences in Peru, gave him a wealth of information upon which to draw when, in later life, he would chronicle the adventures of Hernando de Soto in *La Florida.*

GÓMEZ ARRIVES IN SPAIN

In late summer or early fall of 1560, Gómez arrived in Seville:

> the dark-featured son of Sebastián Garcilaso de la Vega soon would step
> ashore at Seville, where more than thirty years previously his father pre-
> sumably had set forth with the gay caravels of Pedro de Alvarado to
> spread the seeds of Spain and Catholicism while garnering some of the
> silver and gold of the Indies. . . . Gómez now had traced in reverse the
> trail which many conquerors had followed in their search for fulfillment.
> (Varner 198)

Very little is known about Gómez's life in Spain. When he arrived, he traveled to the Spanish province of Extremadura, Captain Sebastián Garcilaso de
la Vega's ancestral homeland, to meet his paternal relatives. Indications are that
these relatives did not receive with great enthusiasm the illegitimate mestizo
son of the illustrious Captain Garcilaso de la Vega. He was accepted by a great-
uncle, Alonso de Vargas y Figueroa of Montilla. He resided in his uncle's home
in Montilla, in the province known as Córdoba. There are strong indications
that being a mestizo was not a social liability there and that he was well accepted by the citizens of the town (Castanien 31).

Although his uncle was a member of the Spanish noble class known as
hidalgos, Gómez was not: "He had no letters patent to qualify him as a hidalgo;
he lacked the income necessary to be enrolled as a *caballero contioso,* that is,
one who, because he was rich enough to outfit himself, was obliged to serve the
king in time of war and who had the privilege of serving on the town council"
(Castanien 33). In keeping with the prevailing customs, because he had no income at that time, Gómez was not allowed to be called a *caballero,* which was
the title given to those in the social class below hidalgo. As a result, he was
considered to be a visitor in the community, but he was allowed to stay because
he was sponsored by his uncle. Gómez's experiences began to improve on September 16, 1561, when his uncle, don Alonso, declared him to be a legitimate
heir of a paternal aunt, Leonor de Vargas.

GÓMEZ SEEKS AN INHERITANCE

In November 1561, Gómez went to the royal court in Madrid hoping to collect
resources based on the elder Garcilaso's services to the Spanish crown. He presented his case to the Council of the Indies. The Council official, García de
Castro, thwarted his hopes. History suggests that the Spanish government
would not relinquish promised compensation to conquest participants when-

ever it could generate a plausible excuse. *The Cambridge History of Latin America* elaborates on this practice:

> Theoretically, the Crown was assigned the role of awarding *encomiendas* [land grants] as a token of gratitude for the recipient's *hazañas* [great deeds] during the conquest or the subsequent early rebellions. In fact, many *conquistadores* [soldiers who participated in the conquest of the Americas] found themselves excluded from the early distributions whereas comparative latecomers who were better connected received handsome grants . . . A man's military record during the conquest, or even his good behavior in office or loyalty to the crown, were at best secondary considerations. (MacLeod 222)

While in Peru as governor, García de Castro had read the accounts about Gonzalo Pizarro's rebellion against the Spanish viceroy and The New Laws, which were recorded in the *Historia general de las Indias* (*General History of the Indies*), the *Crónica del Perú* (*Chronicle of Peru*), and the *Historia del descubrimiento y conquista del Perú* (*History of the Discovery and Conquest of Peru*). The histories that Castro had read recorded that Captain Garcilaso had ample opportunities to escape from Pizarro; since he had not, he should be treated as a traitor. García de Castro claimed this constituted a rebellious act against the king. Young Gómez tried to convince the Council that the historians had given an inaccurate account, but the Council would not accept the explanation. It is quite possible, also, that the elder Garcilaso's association with Alvarado contributed to Castro's opinions. Varner writes:

> Alvarado was beginning to shift his sights to the rich and promising domains of Almagro and Francisco Pizarro. Yet when his new ambitions were made known by jealous associates to the King, they met with immediate disapproval. Nevertheless, Alvarado was able to produce an old capitulation that justified his exploration of southern territory outside the jurisdiction of Almagro and Pizarro, and with this he made haste to depart before a royal order could give him let. And Captain Garcilaso, gambling on his insight, boldly proceeded with this cavalier conquistador, launching upon a voyage which exposed him to the possible disfavor of his sovereign and to the furies of the southern continent. (31)

A NAME CHANGE

Circumstances encountered in Spain caused Gómez to change his name to Garcilaso de la Vega when he was 24 years old. The last time Gómez is known to have used his given name, Gómez Suárez de Figueroa, was in a baptismal record that bore the date November 17, 1563. As Castanien writes,

> On November 22 of that same year, he is identified as Garcilaso de la Vega. Occasionally in later documents, the then familiar Garcilaso de la Vega is accompanied by a statement to the effect that he was formerly known as Gómez Suárez de Figueroa. He did not add the royal title of Inca until later and only in the last few years of his life is the title found consistently as a part of his name. (35)

Biographers agree that it is not clear when Garcilaso de la Vega began to add the title "El Inca" to his name. He had, however, begun to use it by age 51, when *Diálogos del amor* was published in 1590. His name was listed as "Garcilaso Inca de la Vega" on this publication. Some time between age 51 and age 66, when *La Florida* was published in 1605, he began to stress the Inca title in his name. The title page to *La Florida* showed his name sequence to be "El Inca Garcilaso de la Vega." This name sequence was printed in his two subsequent publications, the *Comentarios reales* and the *Historia general del Perú*, completed before he reached the age of 77.

Some historians conjecture that he changed his name because the second son of the prominent Priego family, the elder Garcilaso's maternal relations and the traditional feudal rulers of Montilla, shared the name Gómez Suárez de Figueroa. Others suggest that his family encouraged him to adopt another name because they opposed the Figueroa name being connected with the low social status in which he was trapped (Castanien 35).

GARCILASO JOINS THE ARMY

Around 1564, after the Council of the Indies had ruled against Garcilaso concerning access to compensation, he enlisted in the Spanish army, intending to serve with Don Juan de Austria's unit. There is no evidence that he actually served in this unit. Historians note that Montilla's official records show that he served as a godfather on December 30, 1563, and January 1, 1565. It is possible that these two dates fall just before and just after his service in Don Juan de Austria's unit, but it is more likely that these dates are an indication that, for unknown reasons, Garcilaso never served in Don Juan's detachment.

Other than the time spent on occasional visits to neighboring areas, Garcilaso probably spent the next four to five years exclusively in Montilla. There is ample evidence to suggest that he became a highly regarded member of that community. The local parish records show that he was godfather to several children born in this time period. No one knows with any certainty, however, exactly how Garcilaso spent his time in Montilla. He was interested in horses, and it was at this time that his uncle added additional stalls to the house that he shared with Garcilaso and doña Luisa Ponce de León, Garcilaso's aunt. There is evidence to suggest that he was active in the local church and indications are that he was on very good terms with the local clergy. Historians believe that he probably learned the Italian language on his own initiative at this time.

In December 1567, an uprising of Spanish Arabs, known as Moriscos, began in the Granada province. Sometime between August 1568 and March 1570, Garcilaso rejoined the Spanish army and began a military career in earnest. He spent his own resources to equip himself, as was the custom in that time. Although Garcilaso's resources were limited, there is evidence to suggest that he had the means to outfit himself for the military. He probably had some income from breeding and trading horses, and he had the small inheritance he had received from his father's estate upon embarking for Spain.[10] The king signed three different captain's commissions for Garcilaso on March 4, 1570, June 27, 1570, and August 30, 1570, each of which lasted about two months. Such a commission gave the recipient "permission" to recruit a company of soldiers.

Apparently these commissions held a special significance for Garcilaso. In *La Florida del Inca,* as well as in his publications about Peru, he included the phrase "His Majesty's Captain" after the words "written by the Inca Garcilaso de la Vega." Perhaps he had hoped to carry on the military tradition that had existed in his paternal lineage, or perhaps it was a way to identify with his father and uncles. Indeed, in his compilation *Relación de la descendencia de Garcí Pérez de Vargas* (*Genealogy of Garcí Pérez de Vargas*), published in 1596, El Inca wrote:

> A estos casi ochenta años que mi padre y dos hermanos suyos sirvieron a la Corona de España, quiero añadir los míos, esos pocos e inútiles que en la mocedad serví con espada . . . para que me jactar y ufanas de haberlos imitado en el servir a nuestro Rey, eligiendo por galardón del servicio la gloria de haber cumplido con nuestra deuda y obligación, aunque de todos ellos no poseamos más de la satisfacción de haberlos empleado como se deben emplear y nos basta haber hecho lo que es de nuestra parte. (Garcilaso de la Vega, *Relación,* 238)

> To these almost eighty years, during which my father and his two brothers served the Spanish Crown, I wish to add those few and useless ones

10. Castanien notes that Garcilaso had accumulated enough resources at this point to purchase a slave (30). In addition to the resources listed above, his uncle named Garcilaso the only heir to the estate of his paternal aunt, doña Leonor de Vargas, on September 16, 1561 (33).

that I served with the sword during my youth . . . to boast and brag about the fact that I followed and imitated them in the service of my king, choosing as my reward the fulfillment of our debt and obligation, although for all of it we possess no more than the satisfaction of having spent them as one should, and it is sufficient for us to have done our part. (Garcilaso de la Vega, *Genealogy,* 573)

It is also possible that Garcilaso thought he could gain the respect that the king had continuously refused and at last get his father's service to the Crown legitimized, recognized, and rewarded. The king, however, steadfastly retained his unsympathetic position. El Inca stated that he had enjoyed arms and horses in Cuzco and had continued this involvement after he arrived in Spain:

[S]eríamos de treze o catorze años, nos passamos mis condiscípulos y yo al exercicio de la gineta,[11] de cavallos y armas, hasta que vine a España, donde también ha avido el mismo exercicio, hasta que la ingratitud de algún príncipe y ninguna gratificación del Rey me encerraron en mi rincón.[12]

[A]t about thirteen or fourteen years of age, my companions and I learned about the *gineta,* horses and arms, until I came to Spain, where I continued to practice, until the ingratitude of a certain prince and rejection from the King shut me in my corner.

El Inca's perceptions about the king's actions toward himself and the elder Garcilaso left him emotionally impoverished as long as he lived. The only way that he could extricate himself was to somehow, sometime, gain the respect and recognition that he believed the Crown owed his father for his service. He continued the struggle. His army career ended, Garcilaso returned to Montilla, where his only support was his uncle, Alonso de Vargas.

GARCILASO BEGINS TO WRITE

It seemed Garcilaso always read as an escape, as entertainment, and to occupy his time. It is believed that this was the time in which he began reading the Italian-language book *Dialoghi di amore* (*Dialogues of Love*), by León el Hebreo. He began translating it as he read, and he showed his translation to friends,

---

11. This is a reference to the riding style of the Spanish cavalry, from about the sixteenth to seventeenth century, which they adapted from the cavalry of the Moslem armies that occupied the Iberian Peninsula from A.D. 711 to A.D. 1492.

12. The quotation is from El Inca's letter to Juan Fernández Franco in Asensio.

who encouraged him to continue his work, because they believed it would be well received. No one knows how he became acquainted with Hebreo's book, but he probably had not encountered it before his attempt at a military career.

In 1570, Garcilaso's uncle died. In 1571, Garcilaso also lost his mother, Chimpu Ocllo. He had said good-bye to her when he was twenty, leaving her behind in Cuzco when he sailed to Spain hoping to better his life with the inheritance he thought would be his. It had been twelve years since he last saw her; in 1571 he had to accept the news that he would never see her again. In her will, his mother stated that she had two daughters and she mentioned her son, Gómez Suárez. Later in his life, Garcilaso would express his belief that his Indian mother was a noble person because her ancestors had been Peru's earliest rulers and that the only thing that had enhanced her nobleness was her accepting the Catholic faith. Perhaps his later determination to write about his mother's people was a way to lessen the sense of loss created when he left his mother at such a young age. His writing may have been a way to bring himself spiritually closer to the Palla and her people.

Throughout his life, Garcilaso read a wide variety of literary works, including the chivalrous romances that were popular in Spain when he was a young man; he abandoned reading these works of fiction after reading Pedro Mexía's *Historia imperial y cesárea* (*Imperial History of the Caesars*) (1545), which gave him a desire to read about real happenings. He immersed himself in scholarly pursuits because "by then, the Renaissance ideal of the joint pursuit of arms and letters, already typified by his glorious namesake, had captivated his spirit" (Brading 256). Since he had already tried the "arms" and had not been successful at it, between 1570 and 1586 he began concentrating on "letters" and settled in to his literary and writing career (Castanien 38). Garcilaso had taught himself Italian and had acquired library holdings that indicated he had read works by Renaissance writers, as well as classical Greek and Roman writers. He was proficient in the Quechua language, taught to him by his mother and her relatives, and he spoke and wrote eloquently in the Spanish taught to him by the priest Cuellar. His years in Montilla must have been very productive.

Castanien writes that Garcilaso had a close relationship with the clergy in Montilla and that he had contact with the Jesuits both in Peru and in Spain (36). The order operated a school in Montilla, and it is probable that Garcilaso was in close touch with them. Although Garcilaso is silent upon this matter, Castanien believes he may have begun to improve the education he received in Peru, which he considered sketchy and inadequate, by studying with the Jesuits. Castanien believes also that Garcilaso was encouraged to continue his studies and to write by his acquaintances among the clergy in Montilla. His associations with the Jesuits continued after Garcilaso relocated to Córdoba. Garcilaso received help and encouragement, also, among certain scholars. In a letter to

Juan Fernández Franco, he makes reference to the *Dialogues* and his standing among his fellow scholars: "la qual obra, aunque yo no puse nada en ella sino muchas imperfeccions, ha causado que v.m. y otros señores míos me favorez-can, como me favorescen, sin que en mí aya de escuelas más que el perpetuo desseo dellas" (Asensio 585) ("this literary work, although I did not put much into it other than imperfections, has caused you and other gentlemen to favor me, as do others, without my having much education other than the perpetual desire for it"). One can see from this quotation more evidence that Garcilaso felt his formal education to be inadequate, explaining the motivation behind his continual desire for self-improvement. He stated that one learned scholar, Ambrosio de Morales, adopted him as a son (Castanien 49).

Garcilaso initiated his literary career by heeding the advice he had received to complete translating the *Dialoghi di amore*. When he translated the book, he recorded in the introduction that he considered his native language to be Quechua. The *Dialoghi* was well known by the Italians, but it was not well known to the Spanish. Garcilaso related an interesting conversation with a certain person at the cathedral at Córdoba who had seen his translation and wanted to converse with him about it. Garcilaso stated that he was intimidated about appearing before "tan gran personaje" ("such a great person") (*Historia general* 13). When he eventually agreed to meet with him, Garcilaso stated about his admirer:

Hízome mucha merced en todo, aunque estaba en la cama tullido de gota, y las primeras palabras con que me saludó fueron estas: "Un antártico nacido en el Nuevo Mundo, allá debajo de nuestro hemisferio y que en la leche mamó la lengua general de los indios del Perú, qué tiene que ver con hacerse intérprete entre los italianos y españoles, y ya que presumió serlo por qué no tomó libro cualquiera y no el que los italianos más estimaban y los españoles menos conocían." (*Historia general* 14)

He received me graciously, although he was bedridden with gout, and the first words with which he greeted me were these: "An antarctic born in the New World, below our hemisphere, and one who in his mother's milk received the language of the Indians of Peru, why should you make yourself an interpreter between the Italians and the Spanish, especially since you chose not just any book to translate, but one which the Italians esteem most and the Spanish know least."

The book contains three dialogues: the nature and essence of love, its universality, and its origins. These explain that the basis for all types of love is love of God, which is also the basis for all good and honest deeds. Love of God should exceed all other types of love, but the extent to which the human mind can express love of God depends upon the mind's capacity to comprehend the greatness of God, in whom resides all wisdom and virtue.[13] It was this ideology that Garcilaso found so appealing.

Although Garcilaso had begun reading Hebreo's *Dialoghi* as a leisure activity, very quickly he became captivated by its philosophical discussion of Neoplatonic love, perhaps because it agreed with his own beliefs. He stated that he enjoyed the *Dialoghi* because of the "dulçura y suavidad de su Philosophía"[14] ("sweetness and smoothness of its philosophy"). He agreed with Hebreo's Neoplatonic view of the universe, his belief in man's progression from barbarism and paganism to knowledge of the true God, the idea of order and harmony, and the work of the divine will in the world (Castanien 55).

Garcilaso was the third person to translate this book into Spanish. Apparently he was unaware that it had been translated twice before. One translation was published anonymously in Venice in 1568. The other was translated by Carlos Montesa in 1582 and was published in Zaragoza. Garcilaso had planned a second edition of his translation but was stopped by the Office of the Inquisition. Castanien points out:

> The *Dialogues,* in all editions and in all languages, were entered in the *Index librorum prohibitorum et expurgatorum* of 1612. They were listed in the second class, which excluded certain authors' works that were prohibited or to which words of caution or explanation were to be added. In his remarks concerning a possible second edition, Garcilaso says nothing about amending the text to take care of the objections of the inquiry, whatever they were. (54–55)

Garcilaso's version is widely considered by scholars to be the best translation. Castanien writes, "Menendez y Pelayo, the nineteenth-century dean of Spanish letters who was by no means always so kind to Garcilaso, judges Garcilaso's work to be far superior to that of his predecessors" (54). Critics attribute the superior quality of Garcilaso's translation to his linguistic skill, his comprehension of the philological discourse in the original, and his ability to translate it into the Spanish language. All that was contained in the original was easily accessible to his readers. Varner observes that the accessibility of the translation is due to Garcilaso's scrupulous care to keep the meaning the original author intended:

13. This synopsis is based on the 1960 edition of the *Diálogos* from *Obras completas.*
14. Quotation from the *Obras completas.*

He spent many hours correcting errors made in bringing the text from its original mold, and he passed much more time in an effort to remold the feeling and the sense into Castilian without distorting the Tuscan forms. . . . Aware of the author's purpose and technique, Garcilaso felt that to alter the subtleties and inventions of León Hebreo would be to divorce the context from the art and to deprive the author of the honor due his ability to enclose an elevated doctrine in a vulgate language; he also felt that to add superfluities would be equally disastrous since they would render sublime documents commonplace and rob an equally elevated rhetoric of its subtlety. (279–80)

After completing the *Dialogues* translation in 1586, El Inca began his original writings. It is at this point in Garcilaso de la Vega's life that scholars can safely and accurately call him "El Inca," knowing that he signed the *Dialogues* with the title "Garcilaso Inca de la Vega." He next began recording his interpretation of Hernando de Soto's tragic expedition to southeastern North America, naming the book *La Florida del Inca* (*The Florida of the Inca*).

ARMADA SERVICE INTERRUPTS GARCILASO'S ORIGINAL WRITING

Circumstances beyond his control, however, soon interrupted his writing. In 1588 El Inca traveled to Lisbon to join the famous Spanish Armada (*armada,* "fleet"), commissioned by Philip II to travel to England and end Protestantism forever. He served in the rank of captain of the army unit stationed on the hospital ship *San Francisco.* El Inca also held the rank of *tercio,* an officer who commanded several infantry companies, according to the *Relación verdadera del armada que el rey nuestro señor mandó juntar en el puerto de la cuidad de Lisboa en el reyno de Portugal en el año 1588* (*True Story of the Fleet That Our Lord the King Ordered to Gather at the Port of Lisbon in the Kingdom of Portugal in the Year 1588*) (see Crowley 6). The *San Francisco* did not participate in the Armada campaign because a severe storm hit the Spanish coast between July 12 and July 20. King Philip had ordered the *San Francisco* to set sail on July 16 or the following Sunday. After the storm, forty ships were scattered, and their locations were not known. El Inca's ship was the *almiranta,* the last ship in a convoy, in a fleet that was commanded by Agustín Mexía. Almost all Mexía's fleet, including the *San Francisco,* arrived in Santander after the Armada campaign. Little documentation exists about why they did not participate, but it is assumed that the Armada left so hastily that Mexía's ships did not have time to rejoin the fleet after the storm.

El Inca, himself, never said anything about his participation in the Armada, because, according to Crowley, "it was an Inca custom not to concentrate on the negative aspects of life and battles, but to simply move beyond them, which he did" (8). Crowley also suggests that El Inca was influenced by the Inca custom of relating history by omitting what was considered negative and relating only the positive aspects of an event. The Incas sought to reduce history to its simplest terms so it could be comprehended easily and retained. Since the British won the battle with the Spanish Armada and chased it into the north Atlantic, where it was caught in the currents, carried beyond England and Ireland, and sunk by the rough waters, El Inca may have felt nothing positive could be said and, adhering to Inca custom, chose to omit any reference to it.

At this point in his life, El Inca's thoughts returned to Cuzco and Peru. While he was in Seville on June 27, 1563, he had applied for royal permission to return to Peru; however, he never made the trip, either because permission was denied or because he reconsidered (Castanien 34). This incident is another example of how Garcilaso's mestizo heritage pulled and pushed him two ways at once. All his life, excluding the short time his parents spent together, he was required to abandon half his heritage to embrace the other half. His marginalization in colonial society caused him to view the colonial social order as both an outsider and as an insider. In Spain, El Inca was socially marginalized because, as a mestizo, he could never be considered a full Spanish citizen, nor would his abilities be fully appreciated. The criticism he received from the unnamed scholar at the cathedral of Córdoba regarding his attempt to translate the *Dialoghi* is a good example of the prevailing attitude of his day. While he might have found more social acceptance in Peru, he was physically marginalized from his native land by distance and politics. Varner reflects on El Inca's situation when he observes that, in sixteenth-century European society, El Inca was "an alien, barred by the forged iron bands of a social code" causing the mestizo "always to seek a sense of family and belonging" (278).

EL INCA RESUMES WRITING

After the Armada experience, El Inca returned home and resumed writing *La Florida del Inca,* which he then published in Lisbon in 1605 through the publishing house owned by the Dutch immigrant Pedro Crasbeeck, known as the House of Pedro Crasbeeck. The work is a year-by-year account of the de Soto expedition. El Inca's approach to relating the narrative of the expedition is analyzed in the remaining chapters of this study.

In 1609, El Inca published his best-known work, the *Comentarios reales de los Incas.* This book established him as one of the best contemporary historians of the Quechua people of South America, known collectively to the Europeans as the Incas. The *Comentarios* consists of nine volumes. Book I contains a geographical description of Peru and biographical information on the first emperor (Inca) of the Quechua empire, Manco Capac. With his description of this period of Inca history, we see—as in *La Florida*—El Inca's use of the Platonic concept of the golden age before society was corrupt, a rhetorical device that was popular in the sixteenth and seventeenth centuries. El Inca describes Manco Capac as a messianic person who leads his people from a state of barbarism to enlightenment, ushering in the golden age of the Incas. Book II discusses the religious traditions of the Incas and Book III talks about emperor Mayta Capac extending the Inca empire. Book IV covers women's status within the empire. El Inca places particular emphasis on women's roles in Inca religious life—particularly those who were participants in the Temple of the Virgins. He also discusses at length the Inca marriage ceremonies. Books V, VI, and VII cover Inca agriculture and monetary policies, the emperor Inca Pachacutec and his benevolent tenure in office, and administrative law and Tupac Inca Yupanqui's reign. Book VIII treats Huayna Capac's reign as emperor, and Book IX describes the power struggle between Atahualpa and Huáscar, which led to the destabilization that allowed the subsequent destruction of the empire by Pizarro and his forces.

Until the second half of the eighteenth century, the *Comentarios* was recognized as the best source of information on the Inca empire. According to Zamora, El Inca's knowledge about the Incas was unquestioned (4). Zamora notes, however, that the historian William Robertson, in his book *The History of America* (1777), began to question El Inca's historical veracity by noting that the *Comentarios* was a mixture of fantasy and reality (5). The American historian William Prescott also questioned the historical veracity of El Inca's book when he stated, "his work is the source of most of the facts—and the falsehoods—that have opened speculation in respect to the ancient Peruvians. Unfortunately, at this distance and time, it is not always easy to distinguish the one from the other" (899). Prescott's comments are ironic, however, because his account was based largely on El Inca's book. With regard to Spanish critics reviewing El Inca's works, the most notable has been Menéndez y Pelayo. Zamora tells us that Pelayo believed the *Comentarios* was more a utopian novel, in the tradition of Plato, than a work of history (95). The Peruvian historian González de la Rosa was even more severe in his criticism when he called El Inca a "plagiarizer who had lifted the better part of his history of the Incas from secondary sources" (qtd. in Zamora 5). By contrast, however, other Peruvian scholars such as Quesada, Sánchez, Durand, and Barrenechea have praised the historical qualities of El Inca's work and have pointed out in particular his accuracy, integrity, and objectivity (Zamora 5).

El Inca's idealized depiction of the Incas has, however, undermined his credibility as a historian. Given the apparent historical distortion, this history of the Incas must be viewed more as a literary work than as a historical work. The fact that it is not "historical" in the strict sense of the word does not, however, diminish its overall value. In fact, as Pupo-Walker notes:

> En sus postulados fundamentales la lingística moderna considera al cuento intercalado como una ampliación de las relaciones sintácticas que se dan en los esquemas de las oraciones coordinadas y subordinadas. . . . El conjunto de inserciones narrativas que nos revelan los *Comentarios reales* . . . ponen al descubierto los aspectos más íntimos de la historia; aspectos que no abarcarán nunca el discurso impersonal de la crónica. Me parece . . . además, en que la narración interpolada desarrolla . . . una función perfectiva ya que al mismo tiempo sintetiza el discurso y aproxima los hechos al lector. (191–93)

> In its fundamental principles, modern linguistics considers the inserted narrative to be an amplification of the syntactical relationships that appear in structures of coordinated and subordinated sentences. . . . The narrative insertions that we see in the *Royal Commentaries* . . . reveal to us the most intimate aspects of history; aspects that would not stand out in the impersonal discourse of an ordinary chronicle. It seems to me . . . that interposed narrative performs a perfective function because it synthesizes the discourse and makes the events seem more real to the reader.

This aspect of the "cuento intercalado" is characteristic of all of El Inca's work, because he is trying to do more than simply relate facts. He is writing from a particular perspective that is unique among the chroniclers, and he wants his readers to understand this perspective so that they might have insight into what El Inca believes is the reality of the colonial experience, as well as the causes and potential remedies for that reality. El Inca, then, is attempting to present the story behind the story, in addition to the import of the events he describes. It is precisely this aspect of El Inca's writing that this study of *La Florida del Inca* will explore.

Historia general del Perú, El Inca's last publication and the sequel to the *Comentarios*, was completed at least a year before its publication in 1617. In this publication, he states that his motivation for writing the last work was to praise the heroism of the Spanish soldiers, who, "con su valor y ciencia militar ganaron para Dios, su rey y para sí aquese rico imperio cuyos nombres, dignos de cedro, viven en el libro de la vida y vivirán inmortales en la memoria de los mortales" (12) ("with their valor and military science won for God, their king, and for themselves that rich empire, and whose names, worthy of remembrance, live in the book of life and will live immortal in the memory of mortals"). Typical of El Inca, he seeks to balance his praise of his mother's culture in the *Comentarios* with an equally enthusiastic volume about the exploits of his father and his father's comrades-in-arms in their conquest of Peru. Similar in format to the *Comentarios,* this work is divided into eight books. In Book I, El Inca reminds the reader of the end of the *Comentarios,* then proceeds to narrate the history of the Spanish conquest and to pay tribute to Francisco Pizarro and his family. Book II narrates the arrival of Pedro de Alvarado and his companion, Captain Sebastián Garcilaso de la Vega, in Peru. El Inca discusses the agreement between Alvarado and Diego de Almagro and the death of Alvarado. Book III is a description of the power struggle among the conquerors, resulting in the arrival of the first viceroy, Blasco Núñez de Vela, in an attempt to enforce The New Laws, which are the subject of Book IV. Book V focuses on the priest Pedro de la Gasca and his tenure as president of the *Audiencia,* including his success in putting down the revolt of Gonzalo Pizarro and implementing The New Laws. Book VI narrates Gasca's attempts to keep order after executing Gonzalo Pizarro. Book VII treats the tenure of the viceroy Francisco Hernández Girón, and the *Historia* concludes with descriptions of the rules of three more successive viceroys, Andrés Hurtado de Mendoza, the Marqués de Cañete, and Francisco de Toledo, all of which make up Book VIII.

According to Zamora, El Inca's attempts at corrective history in the *Historia general* are among the most radical examples of revisionist historiography (41). The figures of both the Spanish and the natives are portrayed in epic proportions. El Inca's narrative relies on oral history, with anecdotes added to corroborate the testimony of the eyewitnesses.

Zamora believes El Inca's preoccupation with portraying the figure of the Amerindian as a *caballero* equal to his Spanish counterpart compromises historical veracity in his work (42). The literary ability of the New World's first mestizo writer, however, causes him to stand out as one of the prominent figures of colonial Spanish American literature. Rafael Lapesa makes the case for history as literature by stating:

La pasión, tan dañina para la imparcialidad, ha inspirado muchas de las más bellas páginas de la historia. Hay en la historia ciencia y arte. La parte científica consiste en puntualizar los hechos y sus causas. La artística comprende la presentación de sucesos, personajes y sociedades con vida y relieve, en lenguaje atractivo. (188)

Passion, so detrimental to impartiality, has inspired many of the most beautiful descriptions of history. There is in history science and art. The scientific part consists of enumerating the events and their causes. The artistic part consists of presenting events, characters, and societies in a vivid and attractive way.

Lapesa continues by pointing out that a fine writing style is not only present in works of history but also has at times been more highly valued by society than the history that the authors relate: "la elaboración artística de la exposición apenas cabe en los trabajos eruditos, pero es condición deseable en la historia propiamente dicha; ha habido épocas en que se le ha dado más importancia que al aspecto científico" (188) ("artistic elaboration scarcely appears in erudite literature, but it is a desirable characteristic for a history; there have been epochs in which this was considered more important than the scientific aspect"). The time of El Inca is, without a doubt, one of the "épocas" that can be included in Lapesa's allusion to times when the "elaboración artística" was more important than historical fact. El Inca combined accounts about what he had witnessed with accounts told to him by conquest participants, and these became his three highly regarded chronicles.

EL INCA'S LAST YEARS

El Inca relocated to Córdoba sometime between 1590 and October 11, 1591, when he sold his uncle's house in Montilla, and he spent his last years writing (Varner 301). Never ordained, he became a Catholic lay worker with the title of chaplain, a post inherited from his childless uncle. In 1592 El Inca was appointed *mayordomo* (administrator) of the hospital of the Immaculate Conception of Our Lady in Córdoba. In 1615, he was struck with a severe illness, which left him unable to write because it caused his hand to tremble (Castanien 50).

On April 22, 1616, seventy-eight years plus ten days after it began, El Inca's life ended. He left his possessions to his only known child, a son who had resulted from a common-law relationship he apparently had with his housekeeper, Beatríz de la Vega. Castanien reports:

> In 1930, there was found a copy of some of the treatises of Fray Bartolomé de las Casas, the Dominican Bishop of Chiapas known as the Apostle of the Indies. The book contained two hand-written statements relative to Garcilaso. One owner, Diego de Córdoba, noted that the book was particularly valuable to him because it had belonged to Garcilaso. The second lengthy note was written in 1653 by don Diego's son, Iñigo de Córdoba Ponce de León, who had more interesting information. He identifies the first note as having been written by his father, then adds, "He was an intimate friend of the said Inca Garcilaso de la V. He was truly a man of

very good parts and holy life, he was wise and prudent. . . . I knew him and remember him very well. He was of average height, dark, very quiet in his speech. He had in Spain a son whom I knew very well and who resembled his father." (39)

In 1946, a document was located in the archives in the cathedral chapter of Córdoba that refers to Diego de Vargas as the "natural son of Garcilaso de la Vega" (Castanien 40). It is recorded that on March 31, 1620, Diego de Vargas appeared before the chapter and identified his parents as Garcilaso and Beatríz de la Vega. El Inca referred to Beatríz as a servant, and he referred to his son as "a citizen of Córdoba whom I have brought up" (qtd. in Castanien 40). This was in sharp contrast to Captain Sebastián Garcilaso's words about El Inca when he stated, "such is my will because of the love I have for him being, as he is, my natural son and as such I name and declare him" (qtd. in Castanien 40).

The inscription on the wall of El Inca's commemorative chapel, which he commissioned to be built inside the cathedral of Córdoba, states that he was remembered by his peers as "a renowned man . . . accomplished in letters, valiant in arms, son of Garcilaso de la Vega . . . and of Elizabeth Palla, sister of Huayna Capac, last emperor of the Incas. He commented upon Florida, translated León Hebreo and composed the *Comentarios Reales*" (qtd. in Castanien 50). He was known as an authority on American affairs, particularly Peruvian affairs, and on the customs among the natives in Florida.

It cannot be ignored that on this same day, April 22, 1616, the world lost two other great writers—Miguel de Cervantes and William Shakespeare. Too interesting to be ignored are other similarities between Cervantes and El Inca. Cervantes published his greatest work, *Don Quijote de la Mancha*, in 1605, the same year El Inca published his first original work, *La Florida del Inca*. Both authors rejected the popular sixteenth-century practice of reading novels of chivalry. El Inca stated in *La Florida:*

> Por lo cual, con verdad podré negar que sea ficción mía, porque toda mi vida (sacada la buena poesía) fui enemigo de ficciones, como son libros de caballería, y otras semejantes. Las gracias de esto debo dar al ilustre caballero Pedro Mejía de Sevilla, porque con una reprehensión, que en la *Heroica obra de los Césares* hace, a los que se ocupan en leer y componer los tales libros, me quitó el amor que como muchacho le podía tener, y me hizo aborrecerlos para siempre. (314)

> Therefore, I can with truth deny that mine is fiction, because all my life— except for good poetry—I have been the enemy of fictions such as books of chivalry and other like ones. Thanks for this I must give to the illus-

trious knight Pedro Mejía of Seville, because with a rebuke, which in the *Heroica obra de los Césares* he gave those who occupy themselves in reading and composing such books, he freed me of the love which as a boy I had for them and made me abhor them forever. (176)

Cervantes expressed the same disdain by satirizing books of chivalry and those who read them in his *Quijote*. The Spanish royal court refused to grant the recognition that both men sought. Cervantes had been part of the campaign against the Barbary pirates of North Africa and was taken prisoner in the course of one battle. He languished in a North African prison for a number of years awaiting ransom by the Spanish government. The experience left him physically impaired and angry at a political system that, as El Inca observed, frequently rewarded lesser men. Both Cervantes and El Inca had contributed greatly to their country, and neither received adequate compensation for their contributions and sacrifices.

CONTRASTS AND CONTRADICTIONS

It seems that contrasts and contradictions were central to El Inca's life, starting with his parents—the conquered and the conqueror—two people born and reared on separate continents, one with no written language, no transportation, not even a horse or a wheel, the other with a written language, the printing press, ships, conveyances with wheels, and horses. Garcilaso, himself, neither Amerindian nor Caucasian, was given an education that concentrated on neither culture individually, but on both.

As a young adult, he sought his paternal lineage and lived in that world, but at one period in his life, his mother's world beckoned to him and he considered going back to Peru. His life had been both tranquil and chaotic. He had lived in peace and in war. He experienced both acceptance and rejection. He was accepted by his parents, his Catholic teachers, and associates and rejected by the Spanish nobility, both in Cuzco and in Spain. He had experienced failure and success. He had not accomplished in his early life the things that had been so important to him but had succeeded in a writing career that he had not sought early on: "He was torn between his sympathetic, romantic attachment to an Indian tradition, destroyed by European power and his wish to become a part of that destructive power. He was both the victor and the vanquished, the master and the slave, the oppressor and the victim" (Castanien 146).

Castanien states that the recorded business transactions involving El Inca while he lived in Montilla were that the town council chose a horse he had bred as an approved sire and that El Inca purchased a mulatto slave for sixty ducats. One has to wonder how El Inca reconciled owning a slave with his Christian beliefs and with his passionate advocacy to teach Christianity to the New World natives. In all his writings about the Native Americans, he tries to convince his European readers that Amerindians are, in their own way, as intelligent and as respectable as Spaniards. The contrast that he creates between an Amerindian's humanity and a mulatto slave's humanity contradicts his avowed belief in Christian principles and the philosophies in the Neoplatonic *Dialogues* that he considered so appealing.

2

Purpose, Style, and Themes of La Florida del Inca

Primary concentration in this chapter is upon El Inca's concerns about his writings. An overview about the style in which he writes and why he began to write will be given, also. El Inca's balancing act between his two cultures—Native American and European—will, again, become obvious as he selects and records historical accounts about the de Soto expedition into La Florida, enabling us to see the way in which ethnicity determines certain characteristics of El Inca's approach to the information he relates.

El Inca starts Book I, Chapter I of *La Florida del Inca* by stating that he wants to honor "la Santísima Trinidad, Dios Nuestro Señor" (251) ("the Most Holy Trinity, God Our Lord"; 61) and that is why he is attempting to record the story of Hernando de Soto and "la de muchos otros caballeros e indios" (251) ("that of many other Spanish gentlemen and Indians"; 61). He states that "entonces no entendiesen los españoles sino en descubrir nuevas tierras" (252) ("the Spaniards of that time thought of nothing except the discovery of new lands"; 63).

SPANIARDS WHO EXPLORED LA FLORIDA

All Spanish explorers who went to Florida were carried to their landing spots by prevailing winds. Some landed at unintended places because storms intervened to set them on a new course. In such a storm, El Inca relates, Ponce de León, the governor of Puerto Rico, stumbled upon a strange coast north of the island of Cuba in 1513:

> [L]os indios fabulosamente decían había una fuente que remozaba a los viejos, en demanda la cual anduvo muchos días perdido, sin la hallar. Al cabo de ellos, con tormenta, dio en la costa al septentrión de la isla de Cuba, la cual costa, por ser día de Pascua de Resurrección cuando la vio,

la llamó Florida, y fue el año de mil y quinientos y trece, que según los computistas se celebró aquel año a los veinte y siete de marzo. (253)

[A]ccording to the fables of the Indians, there was a fountain that rejuvenated the aged. Juan Ponce de León wandered fruitlessly for many days seeking this land, and eventually was driven by storm to a coast that lay north of the island of Cuba. This coast he named Florida because it was Easter Day when he first came upon it. The year was 1513, and according to some experts, Easter was celebrated [that year] on the twenty-seventh of March. (64)

Varner and Varner note in their annotated translation of *La Florida* that Ponce de León named the land he had discovered "La Florida" for two reasons: because it was a land of many varieties of flowers and because he and his crew had made landfall on Easter (8). In Spain, Easter was called the day of Pascua Florida. *Pascua* is the common name given to the three great feasts of the year, Whitsunday, Christmas, and Easter. Easter was referred to as Pascua Florida because in Spain flowers usually appear at that time of the year.

León was too excited to wait around to see whether the land they encountered was an island or a larger land area; "vino a España a pedir la gobernación y conquista de aquella tierra" (253) ("he came to Spain to ask for the government and conquest of that country"; 64). After securing permission for the conquest of La Florida from "Los Reyes Católicos,"[15] León set out with three ships and an expeditionary force in "el año de quince. Otros dicen que fue el de veinte y uno. . . . que sea el un año o el otro, importa poco" (253) ("he went thither . . . in the year '15; others say that it was in '21. Whether it was the one year or the other matters little"; 64). After stopping in Cuba to resupply the ships, they set out again and arrived back in La Florida in 1521.

El Inca states that when the León expedition landed in Florida:

Los indios salieron a recibirle, y pelearon con él valerosamente hasta que le desbarataron y mataron casi todos los españoles que con él habían ido, que no escaparon más de siete, y entre ellos Juan Ponce de León; y heridos se fueron a la isla de Cuba donde todos murieron de las heridas que

---

15. Literally, "the Catholic kings," the term used by El Inca and his contemporaries to refer to King Ferdinand and Queen Isabella of Spain. They carried this title in recognition of the fact that their armies drove the last Moslems from the Iberian Peninsula in 1492. Soon after, they expelled, converted to Catholicism, or executed all Spanish Jews, completing what contemporaries saw as a process of making Spain a totally Catholic country.

llevaban. Este fin desdichado tuvo la jornada de Juan Ponce de León, primer descubridor de La Florida, y parece que dejó su desdicha en herencia a los que después acá le han sucedido en la misma demanda. (253)

[T]he Indians came out and fought valiantly until they had defeated him. He himself escaped with only six of his companions . . . they sailed for the island of Cuba, where all died of the wounds they had received. Thus unhappily ended the expedition of Ponce de León, the first to explore the land of Florida, and it would appear that he left his misfortune as a heritage to those who succeeded him in this same search. (64)

These difficulties did not deter others who had participated in explorations in Mexico and Central and South America. Restless and not content to settle themselves in Spain or elsewhere, they heard about La Florida and set their sights upon North America.

Lucas Vásquez de Ayllón, a long-standing judge of the Appellate Court and later a judge of the *Audiencia* in Santo Domingo, along with seven other rich men, organized the second expedition. Ayllón led the expedition in 1524. In 1521, Ayllón and his crew had been on a raiding expedition to capture and enslave Native Americans to work their gold mines and had landed by chance at a cape, which they called Santa Elena. They stumbled upon a river they called Jordan, "a contemplación de que el marinero que primero lo vio se llamaba así" (253) ("in memory of the sailor who first saw it"; 64). This incident invoked the "heritage" of Ponce de León, because, when the 1524 Ayllón expedition landed in the same general area where they had attempted to enslave the natives, the natives remembered the tricks the Spaniards had used to capture them, and they gave the Spaniards the same treatment. The judge and his men returned to Santo Domingo "rotos y desbaratados" (254) ("broken and defeated"; 66).

Pánfilo de Narváez led the next expedition to Florida in 1528. He was accompanied by Alvar Núñez Cabeza de Vaca, who acted as treasurer of the royal purse. Narváez led his expedition so far inland that the crews on the resupply ships waiting on the coast became weary and left before the expedition returned. Without supplies, Narváez and his men built replacement ships from the forest trees and set out across the Gulf toward Mexico. The ships encountered storms, and everyone except Cabeza de Vaca, three other Spaniards, and an African slave were lost. They, too, experienced the heritage of Ponce de León.

Hernando de Soto led the next expedition to Florida in 1539. Since they did not know the extent of the land known as La Florida, de Soto and his men always considered themselves to be in that territory during their exploration, until they arrived in the territory of what they knew to be Mexico. Thus, the La Florida of which El Inca speaks includes the entirety of southeastern North America, from the present state of Florida to Georgia, the Carolinas, Tennessee, Alabama, Mississippi, Arkansas, and west all the way to Texas. It is important to note that El Inca is writing about a region that, at the time of his writing, was still largely unexplored by Europeans. This fact gives him much more creative freedom than he would have had were he to describe a region that was more well known in Europe. El Inca is aware of this as he points out to his readers:

> La descripción de la gran tierra Florida será cosa tan dificultosa poderla pintar tan cumplida como la quisiéramos dar pintada, porque como ella por todas partes sea tan ancha y larga, y no esté ganada ni aun descubierta del todo, no se sabe qué confines tenga. Lo más cierto, y lo que no se ignora, es que el mediodía tiene el mar océano y la gran isla de Cuba. Al septentrión, aunque quieren decir que Hernando de Soto entró mil leguas la tierra adentro, como adelante tocaremos, no se sabe dónde vaya a parar, si confine con la mar o con otras tierras. Al levante, viene a descabezar con la tierra que llaman de los Bacallaos, aunque cierto cosmógrafo francés pone otra grandísima provencia en medio, que llama la Nueva Francia, por tener en ella siquiera el nombre. Al poniente confina con las provincias de las Siete Ciudades, que llamaron así sus descubridores de aquellas tierras . . . Confina asimismo la Florida al poniente con la provincia de los chichimecas, gente valentísima, que cae a los términos de las tierras de México. (252)

> The description of the great land of La Florida will be a difficult thing to depict as completely as we should like to do, for, as it is so extensive and large in every direction, and is not won or even discovered in its entirety, its confines are unknown. What is most certain and not unknown is that to the south lies the Ocean Sea and the great island of Cuba. To the north (although they claim Hernando de Soto went a thousand leagues inland, as we shall tell below) it is not known where it ends—whether it borders upon the sea or upon other lands. To the east it terminates at the land they call Los Bacallaos, though a certain French cosmographer places another extremely large province between, which he calls New France, because of having simply the name there. To the west it borders upon the provinces of the Seven Cities, so called by the discoverers of those lands. . . . La Florida also borders to the west upon the province of the Chichimecas, a most courageous people who live along the limits of the lands of Mexico. (63)

A little later in his narrative, El Inca gives us his thesis statement:

> [F]ue a la Florida el adelantado Hernando de Soto, y entró en ella año de
> '39, cuya historia, con las de otros muchos famosos caballeros españoles
> e indios, pretendemos escribir largamente, con la relación de las muchas
> y grandes provincias que descubrió hasta su fin y muerte, y lo que después
> de ella sus capitanes y soldados hicieron hasta que salieron de la tierra y
> fueron a parar a México. (254)

> [T]he adelantado [explorer] Hernando de Soto went to La Florida, enter-
> ing it in the year '39. His history and that of the many other famous Span-
> ish gentlemen and Indians we are attempting to write at length, together
> with an account of the many and large provinces he discovered up to the
> time of his end and death, and that which his captains and soldiers did
> afterward until they left the land and at length reached México. (67)

El Inca, in his discourse, goes beyond this simple mission, to relate the tale of
a disastrous expedition caused, in large measure, by the haste and arrogance of
de Soto himself. He will show that de Soto fails, time after time, to observe the
disastrous results of the previous expeditions and to take heed of the fact that
these failures resulted from insolent and abusive behavior by the Spanish toward the Amerindians. He, too, will bring upon himself and his men the heritage of Ponce de León. As a result of the failure of the de Soto expedition, the
area known to the Spaniards as La Florida, which El Inca so passionately wanted
Spain to colonize, was settled by other countries and given other names. El
Inca, by using the de Soto expedition as an object lesson, is trying to create a
new paradigm for Euro-Amerindian relations.

THE *CRONISTAS*

While El Inca's purpose in writing about the expedition is unique among *cron-
istas* (chroniclers) of the Indies, his is not the only written account. Besides
La Florida del Inca, there are three known surviving accounts about the human tragedy that was the de Soto expedition to the mysterious, unexplored region known to the Spaniards as La Florida. The first chronicle of the expedition
was published in 1557 by an anonymous Portuguese member of the expedition known as the Fidalgo de Elvas (Gentleman of Elvas). His account, published in Portuguese, is called *Relacao verdadeira dos trabalhos que o governador
D. Fernando de Souto e certos fidalgos portugueses passaram no descobrimiento
da provincia da Flórida (True Relation of the Hardships Suffered by Governor
Hernando de Soto and Certain Portuguese Gentlemen during the Discovery of the*

Province of Florida). Only three copies of the original edition are known to exist. One is at the New York Public Library, another is at the Bibliotheca de Ajuda in Portugal, and the third is at the British Museum. All citations from this chronicle that appear in this analysis are from a scrupulous English translation by James A. Robertson that is included in *The De Soto Chronicles*. This version of the Elvas narrative is valuable for scholarly purposes because "it has stood the test of over fifty years and is still considered to be an excellent translation" (Hoffman 19). The edition printed in *The De Soto Chronicles* in particular is useful to the scholar because the historian John H. Nann has updated Robertson's notes and added notes of his own that provide important historical context for the narrative.

Elvas, the anonymous author's hometown, is located in Portugal near the Spanish border, very close to Badajóz, one of the largest cities in de Soto's home province of Extremadura (Robertson 27). Evidently, Portuguese citizens were not supposed to participate in Spanish expeditions to the New World, but the proximity of Elvas to the border with Spain allowed some Portuguese to secretly volunteer for de Soto's expedition. Robertson, in the introduction to his translation, observes:

> That Portuguese should join the expedition is not at all strange. Badajóz . . . lay near the Portuguese town of Elvas. To this very day, each place is an active smuggling center. Each is a place of entry or departure into or from the other country. There is, and probably always has been, a constant passing from one place to another. Still, the precaution seems to have been taken of enrolling the men who came from Elvas as being of the town of Badajóz—this undoubtedly to satisfy any official inquiry that might be made. (27)

Perhaps this is also the reason the author of this account wished to remain anonymous.

The second account is El Inca's *La Florida del Inca*. The third account appears in the *Historia general y natural de las Indias* (*General and Natural History of the Indies*), by Gonzalo Fernández de Oviedo (1478–1557), the official chronicler of the Indies. This account was transcribed from the first-person account of Rodrigo Rangel, de Soto's personal secretary during the expedition, and chronicles the entire expedition, with the exception of the final year. Oviedo was the first chronicler of the Indies who tried to cover the history of the entire conquest, from 1492 to the Peruvian civil wars. He was constable for many years of the royal fortress at Santo Domingo (today this island is called the Dominican Republic and Haiti), the chief port of entry and exit for the colonies, and he kept detailed records on each part of the Spanish empire, largely based on firsthand accounts of those who were passing through the port. He frequently inserted into his own text the accounts of those who were returning to Spain from New World adventures (Brading 31–32). Oviedo published the first part of his *Historia general* in 1535. This multivolume work describes the events of the conquest up to 1520. He applied for royal permission to publish the remaining part, which details the conquest of Mexico and the Peruvian civil wars, but was denied permission to publish. The text was eventually published by Spain's Royal Academy of History in 1851 (Brading 34). With the publication of this text, Rangel's history of the de Soto expedition became available to the general public for the first time.

The last extant chronicle is a brief testimonial given by the *factor,* or tax collector, of the expedition, Hernández de Biedma. The testimony was given to the Council of the Indies in 1544 but remained unpublished until 1841.

These four chronicles relay the same basic events, but El Inca's imagination and style give the world the longest and best-written chronicle, preferred by literary scholars through the years. El Inca's mestizo status and his contacts with religious leaders within the Catholic faith, combined with his classical, Renaissance, and medieval Spanish reading interests, give him a writing style that is extensive and expansive when compared with the necessarily narrow styles possessed by the other de Soto chroniclers.[16]

WHY EL INCA WROTE

Knowing of El Inca's failure to receive the recognition he desired in the political and military worlds, perhaps the scholar can safely assume that among the initial stimuli for El Inca to write were his circumstances. In the letter to Juan Fernández Franco (Asensio), El Inca asks him to "me trate como a soldado que, perdido por mala paga y tarde, se ha hecho estudiante" ("treat me like a soldier who, lacking compensation, has become a student"). The "adversity of his fortune" left him in the "refuge and shelter of the disillusioned"—solitude and

---

16. Classical, medieval, and Renaissance were the styles that El Inca learned and upon which he based his writings. Each literary and philosophical period in history slowly encroached upon the preceding period until the old gradually gave way to the new, with some overlap and blending occurring at the end and the beginning of each. When the Renaissance replaced the medieval period, the overlapping and blending started in the twelfth century. By the sixteenth century, the Renaissance style was in vogue, retaining only reminiscent characteristics of the medieval period. The Renaissance ("new birth") period is the era in European history in which writers and others once again learned and practiced classical (Greek and Roman) philosophy in science, writing, art, and relationships. El Inca's ancestor, the other Garcilaso de la Vega (1501–1536), the soldier-poet, was the first Castilian to learn the Italian Renaissance literary style. It was he who established it in Spain.

poverty (Castanien 57). In this state, idleness began to erode his emotions. To avoid the consequences of his escape from his bad fortunes into "solitude and poverty," El Inca began his scholarly pursuits.

Secondary to a desire to fill his time and find a constructive alternative to soldiering, another motivating factor in the writing of *La Florida* was El Inca's renewed acquaintance with Gonzalo Silvestre. After Silvestre's deportation to Spain in 1556, probably neither El Inca nor he expected to see each other again. However, their colonial experiences thrust both into social circles that assured they would meet again. El Inca's continually unsuccessful attempts to convince the Council of the Indies to grant his claim to his father's land grants in Peru often brought him to Madrid, where the Council was located. At the same time, Silvestre was serving as an informal advisor to the Council on issues concerning the La Florida expedition and other military campaigns in which he had participated. No one knows exactly when their paths crossed in Madrid, but their eventual chance encounter there renewed their relationship. Castanien speculates about how El Inca got the idea to write about La Florida:

> The French intrusions into Florida must have been a topic of conversation in the Court and it is quite possible that Garcilaso's acquaintance with Silvestre combined with the news of the day, suggested to Garcilaso the possibility of writing a history of the colony based upon the account of an eyewitness to the most extensive exploration of the area that had been made to that date. (65)

With their relationship renewed, El Inca became Silvestre's part-time secretary. This association gave El Inca an opportunity to hear what Silvestre knew about the de Soto expedition. When El Inca began *La Florida del Inca,* Silvestre lived in a nearby village called Las Posadas. To research his project, El Inca would journey there to talk with Silvestre. El Inca often mentions Silvestre in the narrative, but he does not say that Silvestre is his primary source. El Inca states in his introduction to *La Florida* that he relied on the oral history of the old "hombre noble hijodalgo" (247) ("nobleman and hidalgo"; 54). Although El Inca never identified his primary source for *La Florida,* scholars who have studied the book believe that the individual identified in the introduction as a "caballero" (247) ("gentleman"; 53) is the old soldier Gonzalo Silvestre (Castanien 64).

SILVESTRE

Gonzalo Silvestre was born in 1518 in Herrera de Alcántara, in the Cáceres province, which was located in the region in Spain known as Extremadura. He left Spain with Hernando de Soto for La Florida in 1539, when he was approximately twenty years old. When the three-year expedition came to its tragic end, he and the other survivors were able to reach Mexico. After recuperating, Silvestre and other survivors left Mexico and traveled to Peru, while some survivors returned to Spain.

In Peru, Silvestre became involved in the civil wars that were characteristic of the first four decades of the conquest. Always a royalist, he served in the king's armies until all the rebellions ended. Although his loyalty to the Spanish king was always without question, Silvestre did not receive compensation for his loyalty. In 1556, the arrival of a new viceroy, the Marqués de Cañete, cut short Silvestre's appeals. Eager to enrich his friends and relatives through land grants and colonial government positions, Cañete was hostile to Silvestre and the other veterans because they were petitioning for *repartimientos* (land grants). The king had sent Cañete to Peru to see that the provisions in The New Laws were enforced. One provision in these laws stipulated that married settlers would be given priority for land grants. The viceroy offered to grant petitioners' requests if they would agree to marry prostitutes that he had brought with him, knowing that these aristocrats would refuse and he could use this refusal as a pretense to deny their requests. He then invited them to Los Reyes, the colonial governmental center at that time, arrested them, and sent them back to Spain (Castanien 64–66).

Prior to his deportation, Silvestre was a frequent guest in the home of Captain Garcilaso in Cuzco. At this time, El Inca was about thirteen years old. El Inca notes in a document dated April 22, 1616, written in his last hours, that his friendship with Silvestre began around the year 1552 (Varner 115). When socializing, Silvestre liked to tell stories about La Florida and other conquest adventures. Varner explains how and when El Inca's interest in La Florida began:

> He must have fed often at the Garcilaso table, and he must have paid as often for such hospitality with bewitching tales, stories which echoed to the music of trumpet and drum and moved to the rhythm of galloping horses. And though he strayed at times from the truth, he unraveled his experiences with a joyous courage and gave substance to the visions of a *mestizo* who some day would record them. In this felicitous rapport between a boasting New World Quixote and an aspiring Peruvian boy are to be found the seeds of the Inca Garcilaso's account of Hernando de Soto's exploration of those vast regions north of Mexico which the Spaniards since the discoveries of Ponce de León had referred to as La Florida. (115)

Silvestre lived until 1592 and his close friendship with El Inca was the foundation that led to the publication of *La Florida del Inca.*

EL INCA'S OTHER SOURCES

El Inca states in his introduction to *La Florida* that, along with his reliance upon the old *caballero* (knight), he relied upon the written accounts of two other individuals who participated in the de Soto expedition—Alonso de Carmona and Juan Coles. These two written accounts have never been found, and some scholars believe that they never existed. The additional information provided by these supposedly written accounts may very well have been nothing more than El Inca's own embellishments.

Coles reportedly wrote notes about the expedition and gave them to the Franciscan priest Pedro Aguado. According to El Inca, the priest absent-mindedly left these notes at a print shop in Córdoba, where El Inca happened to see them. Carmona reportedly sent his notes to El Inca. Frances G. Crowley states in his biographical sketch about El Inca that the notes reportedly provided by the two soldiers were brief because they had not intended to publish them "under their own names" (14). When considering El Inca's descriptions of La Florida, it is important to remember that he was not a participant in the de Soto expedition and thus had to rely on his own imagination or additional sources to complete any accounts by Silvestre that contained lapses. Crowley continues:

> Indeed, since Juan Coles quoted verbal statements by participants, and since the report was written on legal paper, it might have been part of a legal deposition. Garcilaso claimed that Juan Coles's data agreed with the compilation of evidence gathered in Mexico for Don Antonio de Mendoza, whose papers would contribute greatly to future studies of *La Florida*. (14)

According to El Inca, he included these two accounts to give credibility to his narrative. Castanien notes that El Inca, himself, states that using the narratives of two additional eyewitnesses to the events of the expedition served not only to fill in gaps of information but also to confirm the veracity of his informant's descriptions (67). El Inca's desire for credibility in his narrative caused him to include the material from these two sources, even though, as he states, he acquired them after he completed his initial draft of *La Florida*.

El Inca does not mention the other three written accounts by Elvas, Rangel, and Biedma. It is possible that he did not know of the existence of the accounts by Rangel and Biedma, since these two accounts were not published until the nineteenth century. El Inca might have been aware of the account by Elvas through Gonzalo Silvestre; because Silvestre is virtually ignored in the Elvas narrative, this might have motivated him to work with his literate friend on a different version of the events.

WHY EL INCA WROTE *LA FLORIDA*

In addition to his commitment to tell Silvestre's story, El Inca felt a commitment to tell the story of La Florida for other reasons, as well. As a mestizo, El Inca believed he was obligated to record the heroics both of the Spaniards who were in de Soto's expedition and of the Amerindians whom they encountered in La Florida and not to allow history to exclude the Florida natives. He wanted to record the accounts given about the land and its great potential, which at the time he began to write were generally unavailable to the public, so that the Spanish government would have to agree to its colonization so that the natives could be converted to Catholicism and the Spaniards could settle there. In his own words, he states:

> Conversando mucho tiempo y en diversos lugares con un caballero, grande amigo mío, que se halló en esta jornada, y oyéndole muchas y muy grandes hazañas que en ella hicieron así españoles como indios, me pareció cosa indigna y de mucha lástima que obras tan heroicas que en el mundo han pasado quedasen en perpetuo olvido. Por lo cual, viéndome obligado de ambas naciones, porque soy hijo de un español y de una india, importuné muchas veces a aquel caballero escribiésemos esta historia, sirviéndole yo de escribiente. . . . En la cual historia—sin las hazañas y trabajos que, en particular y en común, los cristianos pasaron y hicieron, y sin las cosas notables que entre los indios se hallaron—se hace relación de las muchas y muy grandes provincias que el gobernador y adelantado Hernando de Soto y otros muchos caballeros . . . descubrieron en el gran reino de la Florida. Para que hoy más . . . se esfuerce España a la ganar y poblar, aunque sin lo principal, que es el aumento de nuestra Santa Fe Católica, no sea más de para hacer colonias donde envíe a habitar sus hijos, como hacían los antiguos romanos . . . porque es tierra fértil y abundante de todo lo necesario para la vida humana, y se puede fertilizar mucho más de lo que al presente lo es de suyo. (247)

> Conversing many times and in various places with a gentleman, a great friend of mine, who was on this expedition, and hearing from him of the many and very great feats that Spaniards and Indians alike performed in the course of it, it seemed to me an unbecoming thing and a great pity that deeds as heroic as any that have taken place in the world should remain in perpetual oblivion. I myself, therefore, being obligated to both nations, because I am the son of a Spaniard and an Indian woman, importuned that gentleman many times that we write this history, I serving him as amanuensis. . . . In this history, besides the exploits and hardships

the Christians performed and passed through, singly and in common, and besides the notable things that were found among the Indians, an account is given of the many and very large provinces the governor and *adelantado* Hernando de Soto and many other gentlemen discovered in the great kingdom of La Florida, in order that henceforth . . . Spain may be obliged to win and settle it, even though, aside from the principal motive, which is the increase of our Holy Catholic faith, it is only to establish colonies where her sons can be sent to live, as the ancient Romans did . . . It is a fertile land abounding in everything necessary for human life, and it may be made much more productive. (53–54)

This language in the preface lends the impression that *La Florida* might be considered seventeenth-century propaganda. Henige lends support to this interpretation when he states that El Inca "hoped to galvanize the Spanish Crown into colonizing and proselytizing Florida" (18). El Inca is probably hoping that, in addition to spurring a colonization effort, his role as the "amanuensis" (scribe) for Silvestre will allow him to achieve fame through his writing. He presents himself to the reader as the go-between that allows the general public to share in the adventures he describes. He wants the reader to believe, as well, that the authorial voice is that of the old "gentleman," while El Inca is merely the one who puts pen to paper. That distinction between author and scribe often becomes less distinct, however, as El Inca lends his own creative touches to the narrative, as we shall see in this analysis.

After El Inca has been persuaded by experiences in his life to begin writing, he states that he receives more satisfaction and recreation for the soul from his writing than from pursuing wealth and that he hopes his works will bring him the honor and fame he seeks (Castanien 61). El Inca writes:

Aunque, mirándolo desapasionadamente, debo agradecerle muy mucho el haberme tratado mal, porque, si de sus bienes y favores hubiera partido largamente conmigo, quizá yo hubiera echado por otoros caminos y senderos que me hubieran llevado a peores despeñaderos o me hubieran anegado en ese gran mar de sus olas y tempestades, como casi siempre suele anegar a los que más ha favorecido y levantado en grandezas de este mundo . . . conosolado y satisfecho con la escaseza de mi poca hacienda, paso una vida, gracias al Rey de los Reyes y Señor de los Señores, quieta y pacífica, más envidiada de ricos, que envidiosa de ellos. (249)

[L]ooking upon it dispassionately, I must thank her (Fortune) greatly for having treated me badly, because, if she had shared her goods and favors generously with me, perhaps I would have set out on other roads and paths which might have carried me to worse precipices or might have annihilated me in that great sea with its waves and storms, as she nearly always destroys those whom she has most favored and raised up in the places of eminence of the world. . . . consoled and satisfied with my scanty means, I lead, thanks to the King of Kings and Lord of Lords, a life quiet and peaceful, more envied by the rich than envious of them. (57)

In addition to seeking fame and solace for himself and recording the deeds of Silvestre, El Inca is preoccupied with presenting the Amerindian as a *caballero* equal to his Spanish counterpart. As Crowley notes, "It was his avowed primary goal to effectively present the Inca cause before the Spanish crown. This purpose is clearly stated in the preface and preambles of most of his works. . . . He was and is among the first and foremost representatives of the *mestizo* viewpoint in the New World" (1).

In *Language, Authority, and Indigenous History in the Comentarios Reales de los Incas,* Margarita Zamora expresses her opinion that equal status is given to both Europeans and Amerindians in El Inca's writings (42). The reader can see that indigenous and European discourses are combined by El Inca, particularly in material related to Native Americans. José Antonio Mazzotti believes there is an "Andean dialogue" in addition to a "European reading" (197–98) of Native American culture in El Inca's works. While Mazzotti applies his analysis to the *Comentarios reales,* this dualism is present in all of El Inca's works, including *La Florida.* The term *Andean dialogue* could just as easily mean Amerindian dialogue, because El Inca realizes that colonial society is neither Spanish nor Native American; rather, it is in the process of integrating both cultures into one. It is this process of integration that he is attempting to influence by posing as the "scribe" for Silvestre. The narrative is Silvestre's, but the thought process at work in relating it to the reader is El Inca's. His mixed ancestry compels him to elevate the Native American to the level of the European, one way or another. He writes in order to "defend the good name of the Indian race" (Brading 256).

His eagerness to equalize the Amerindians with the Spaniards is caused by his self-identification (Castanien 61; Brading 255–57). One can imagine that his mestizo heritage gives him self-opinions that are based on the same concept that he attaches to Native Americans. As a blood relative to the Native Americans, their struggles are his struggles. He seeks on their behalf the things that he seeks on his own behalf. He tries to aid them in their own self-identity and in their struggle to acquire their place in the New World's social order just as he seeks to gain his own acceptance and place. As Mazzotti observes, one can perceive an Amerindian, as well as a European, tone to his writings.

With *La Florida,* in addition to presenting the Florida natives as equal to the Spanish, El Inca is greatly concerned that Spain should give them the same opportunities to convert to Catholicism as had been given to the Peruvian natives, a desire that is evident when he states that "cierto, confesando todo la verdad, digo que, para trabajar y haberla escrito, no me movió otro fin sino el deseo de que por aquella tierra tan larga y ancha se extienda la religión cristiana" (249) ("certainly, stating the whole truth, I say that I was moved by no other purpose in laboring and having written this work than the desire that the Christian religion be extended over such a large and broad country"; 57). He states that he believes the natives in La Florida, like the Peruvian natives, will easily convert because their pagan ceremonies are not numerous (Castanien 63). El Inca describes the natives' religion, while acknowledging that it is pagan and should be replaced, as almost monotheistic and similar in form to Catholicism: "adoran al Sol Y la Luna por principales dioses, más sin ningunas ceremonias de tener ídolos ni hacer sacrificios . . . ni otras supersticiones como la demás gentilidad" (255) ("they worship the sun and the moon as chief deities . . . without ceremonies involving idols, or sacrifices . . . or other superstitions such as heathens practice"; 68).

To convince the Spanish to colonize La Florida as they had colonized Peru and other New World territory, El Inca knows he will have to sell the government on the economic possibilities in the region. Spain had shown no interest in completing the La Florida conquest and colonizing the area. Through the oral and written reports El Inca encounters about the region, he sees La Florida as an area rich in every potential, especially human. He believes that Spain should hasten to colonize La Florida, so that her less religious neighbors, France and England, will not gain the land and corrupt the natives.

WHY EL INCA WROTE AS HE WROTE

In his effort to impart his ideas to the reader, El Inca employs a writing style that is simple and easily comprehended. His two-part education greatly affects his scholarly writings. Crowley notes that El Inca's historical works and viewpoints reflect this two-part and, sometimes, conflicting educational content—the Spanish culture with its Western canon "classics" and the Inca history, tradition, and mythology. El Inca exhibits in his writings that he realizes this, and he attempts to reconcile the two sides because, as he states, he is "obligado de ambas naciones" (247) ("obligated to both nations"; 53). His desire to make his work appealing to the reader lies also in his desire to achieve fame and respect in an era in which writing is the principal means by which an intellectual can achieve these goals.

Max Hernández states his belief that the "complexities and contradictions of the *mestizo* condition in those days, a complicated mixture of conflicting forces and powerful emotions" also contributes greatly to El Inca's literary style and themes (318). El Inca's mestizo status allows him to retain unique perspectives and the ability to be more objective about the conquest and American colonization than his Spanish counterparts. As a mestizo, he could view the colonial experience as a Spaniard, as an Amerindian, and as a person whose heritage allowed, as well as required, him to combine both. His writing style, consequently, gives the appearance of balance and objectivity. El Inca utilizes the critical method and the patriotic-intent style that was used in humanist historiography of the sixteenth century: "Garcilaso thoroughly assimilated both the critical method and the patriotic intent that had animated humanist historiography since the days of Bruni" (Brading 256). These traditions influenced all of El Inca's writings, and their influences on *La Florida* will be explored in Chapters 3 and 4.

Although El Inca's original intent was to write in the historical style, he incorporated such great literary expression as he wrote that he became appreciated as a literary writer as well. El Inca was "both a literary writer and a historical chronicler of the conquest of the Americas" (Crowley 1). That is why we should examine his work in both a literary and a historical context.

Two rhetorical traditions are incorporated by El Inca into his historical narrations.[17] Although these traditions were invented by two cultures on two continents at separate times, upon close examination, it is obvious that both sought the same objective: to describe societies and their actions in a very idealized way. On the Amerindian side, as Crowley notes, "it was Inca custom not to concentrate on negative aspects of life and battles, but to simply move beyond them, which he did" (8). Such negative practices as human sacrifice and tribal-succession wars were not included in El Inca's historical narrations. In Europe, El Inca became acquainted with the prevailing literary practice that one sees in More's *Utopia* (1516), which also idealizes pre-Christian societies as the precursors of Christian civilization. According to this paradigm, pre-Christian societies are to be excused of their paganism since they never had the opportunity to know of Christian doctrine. Their accomplishments, thus, are praiseworthy in spite of their pagan ways. Using this approach to describe to the Catholic world the customs of a pagan civilization, El Inca places the natives of North America within a context that the European reader can understand and, more important, accept. For El Inca, all the characteristics of civilization are present within the Amerindian societies of North America; they need only the enlightening power of Catholicism to reach the same level of civilization as the Europeans (Dowling 118).

---

17. I use the term *rhetorical traditions* because the Incas did not have a written literature prior to colonization, although their oral histories served the same function as books served within the European context; thus, their rhetorical strategies could just as easily be applied to the written word as the spoken word.

To accomplish his literary goals, El Inca combines reality and imagination. He is able to draw upon not only what his informant tells him but also his vast wealth of knowledge accumulated through his experiences and travels, both in Peru and in Spain. El Inca uses his background knowledge to enhance *La Florida* in the style of a novelist. Since El Inca is both novelist and historian, *La Florida del Inca* can best be described as what Lapesa refers to as "historia narrativa" (190) ("narrative history"), which is the artistic presentation of evidence. El Inca employs a number of rhetorical devices typical of European Renaissance writing. For example, he places brilliant oratory in the mouths of his characters. This type of history, according to Lapesa, usually is not "escrupulosa" (190) ("scrupulous") in the sense that historical detail is secondary to giving the reader a true sense of the events and the characters of the persons involved. Another important aspect of the literature of the period as noted by Lapesa is particularly relevant to *La Florida*. He states: "La mayor novedad de la época estuvo a cargo de los historiadores de Indias españoles, que, interesados por las razas, creencias, costumbres y modos de vida de los pueblos indígenas, dieron entrada en la historia a todos estas cuestiones, hasta entonces no tratadas por ella" (190–91) ("The greatest innovation of the period came from the Spanish historians of the Indies, who, interested in the races, beliefs, customs, and lifestyles of the indigenous peoples, addressed all of these questions, which until this time had been ignored by historians").

EL INCA INTERPRETS LA FLORIDA

To achieve his objective of idealizing La Florida, El Inca uses positive adjectives throughout the narrative. At the point in the book when de Soto first lands at his destination, El Inca instantly begins to emphasize the land's natural productivity:

> Surgieron las naos en una bahía honda y buena que llamaron del Spíritu Sancto . . . El primero de junio echaron los bateles a tierra, los cuales volvieron cargados de yerba para los caballos y trujeron mucha agraz de parrizas incultas que hallaron por el monte, que los indios de todo este gran reino de la Florida no cultivan esta planta ni la tienen en la veneración que otras naciones, aunque comen la fruta de ella cuando está muy madura o hecha pasas. Los nuestros quedaron muy contentos de las buenas muestras . . . de tierra por asemejarse en las uvas a España, las cuales no hallaron en tierra de México ni en todo el Perú. (273)

> The vessels anchored in a deep and good bay, which they named El Espíritu Santo . . . On the first of June the small boats went to the shore

and returned laden with grass for the horses, and they brought also many green grapes from the vines they found growing wild in the woods. The Indians of all this great kingdom of La Florida do not cultivate this plant or regard it as highly as do other nations though they eat its fruit when it is well ripened or made into raisins. Our people were much pleased with these good specimens they brought from the land, for they were similar to the grapes of Spain, and they had not found them in the lands of México nor in the whole of El Perú. (99)

In contrast, the other chronicles make no mention of the natural productivity of the area around the "good bay," which is thought to be today's Tampa Bay. In fact, El Inca's description seems to contradict descriptions of the area related in some other narratives, including those about other expeditions to the area. As an example, Alvar Núñez Cabeza de Vaca, who participated in the earlier failed expedition to La Florida led by Pánfilo de Narváez and recounted his adventures in a book called *Naufragios* (*Shipwrecked*) (1542), states that the land appeared to be very poor, with few resources for supporting a colony, and that there was no decent deep-water port (88–89). One reason the Narváez expedition left this bay area and traveled to Apalache was a lack of food. Cabeza de Vaca records that the scarcity of provisions was a continuous problem as they traveled in the area and was exacerbated by constant surprise attacks by the natives (91).

Elvas, like Cabeza de Vaca, tells us that de Soto and his army encountered the same insufficiency of food on their march to Apalache:

There he [de Soto] awaited the men who were coming behind, who were experiencing great hardship from hunger and bad roads, as the land was very poor in maize, low and very wet, swampy, and covered with dense forest, and the provisions brought from the port were finished. Whenever any village was found, there were some blites, and he who came first gathered them and, having stewed them with water and salt, ate them without anything else. Those who could not get any of them gathered the stalks from the maize fields which being still young had not maize, and ate them. (65)

Conversely, El Inca praises the fertility of the land that extended from the bay to Apalache. In the episode about the "Thirty Lancers," El Inca states that the bounty in this area saved de Soto and his men from starvation. With de Soto and his men in a desperate situation, El Inca illustrates how the land's bounty comes to their rescue in an almost miraculous way:

Habiendo caminado seis leguas, le hallaron alojado en unos hermosísimos valles de grandes maizales, tan fértiles que cada caña tenía a tres y a cuatro mazorcas de las cuales cogían de encima de los caballos para entretener la hambre que llevaban. Comíanselas crudas, dando gracias a Dios Nuestro Señor que los hubiese socorrido con tanta hartura, que a los menesterosos cualquiera se les hace mucha. (296)

Having marched six leagues, they found him encamped in some very beautiful valleys having large maize fields, so productive that each stalk had three or four ears, some of which they gathered while mounted on their horses, in order to appease their hunger. They ate them raw, giving thanks to God, our Lord, for having succored them with such abundance, for to the needy anything seems a great deal. (141–42)

El Inca notes that the supply of maize in the area was sufficient to save not only the thirty lancers and de Soto from starvation but also was enough to reprovision the entire expedition (142–46).

Several aspects of El Inca's narrative are similar to those of the other de Soto narratives. He comments on La Florida's dangerous characteristics, such as swiftly flowing rivers, quicksand, and swamps. He points out that the terrain is an obstacle for de Soto and his expedition and aids the natives in their hit-and-run warfare against the Spanish. For example, El Inca describes a river the Spanish encounter in the Indian province of Ocali:

Cerca del pueblo había gran río de mucha agua, que aún entonces, con ser de verano, no se podía vadear. Tenían las barrancas de una parte y otra de dos picas en alto, tan cortadas como paredes. En toda la Florida, por la poca o casi ninguna piedra que la tierra tiene, cavan mucho los ríos y tienen barrancas muy hondas. (299)

Near the pueblo there was a large river, carrying much water, that even then, it being summer, could not be forded. There were precipices on either side as high as the length of two pikes and as perpendicular as walls. Throughout La Florida, because of the almost absence of stone in the country, the rivers cut very deeply and have very steep banks. (148)

In spite of acknowledging the trouble the Spanish encounter with this river, El Inca quickly reverts to his overwhelmingly positive tone by describing the region of Ocali (between the coast and Apalache) as far more hospitable than the coastal regions the Spanish traversed before arriving there. Elsewhere he points out that the quicksand the Spanish had encountered in the salt marshes near the coast does not exist in the region of Ocali. He continues by saying that Ocali is a much more fertile region than the coastal areas (146).

In his zeal to promote the fertility of the region, El Inca's comments appear self-contradictory at times. Commenting on Ocali, he states that de Soto and his men had great difficulty finding supplies of meat because of the scarcity of game in the area. This statement in the narrative seems to contradict the description of the abundance of certain kinds of deer that, according to El Inca, inhabited that same region (146–48).

As an aside, perhaps El Inca's proclamation about large deer in abundance is true and the Spanish soldiers could not happen upon them because their arms and armor clacked and clanged so loudly that the animals were stampeded ahead of them. One can imagine the noise created by the metal-clad men, their horses, and their dogs as they invaded the territories and how it startled the people and animals occupying the land.

Still, even after noting the expedition's inability to find meat, El Inca once again departs from the descriptive paradigm of his fellow chroniclers by devoting several pages to extensive descriptions of the beauty and abundance of La Florida's flora and fauna. He refers specifically to plant life, such as cedar and sweet gum trees, laurels, and abundant walnut trees, as well as junipers, oaks, and pines (148).

While El Inca acknowledges that the next region the Spanish encounter, known as Apalache, is not rich in gold, as was rumored at the time, he, once again, praises the natural abundance of the area and encourages the reader to believe that it is a good site to colonize. His description of the region is much more positive than those of the other chroniclers (253–54). El Inca points out that the flora and terrain would be excellent for growing domesticated crops and supporting domesticated animals, particularly cattle and hogs, because of the large quantities of forage in the area. He concludes this chapter on a positive note by emphasizing the region's "buenas partes" (358) ("good qualities"; 254). This positive attitude toward Apalache stands in marked contrast to the description offered by Cabeza de Vaca, who describes the same region as difficult to traverse and almost devoid of resources (98–99).

One reason for the difference between this description and the one offered by El Inca, other than El Inca's promoting colonization, is Cabeza de Vaca's desire to emphasize his own personal suffering during his misadventures in La Florida, since his goal for writing his book was to promote his standing in Spanish society. In emphasizing the negative aspects of the region, he makes his deeds there look heroic. Juan Francisco Maura notes in a footnote to the Cátedra edition of *Naufragios* that "dicha información no es más que un recurso literario para resaltar la importancia por él [Cabeza de Vaca] realizada en el Nuevo Mundo" (97) ("this information is nothing more than a literary means of emphasizing his [Cabeza de Vaca's] own importance in this New World adventure"). El Inca concludes his Apalache section on a positive note, but Cabeza de Vaca's conclusion about Apalache is overwhelmingly pessimistic: "Dejo aquí de contar esto más largo, porque cada uno puede pensar lo que se pasaría en tierra tan extraña y tan mala, y tan sin ningún remedio de ninguna cosa, ni para estar ni para salir de ella" (103) ("I will not say any more about this, since each person can imagine what we endured in this land that was so strange and so bad, and so lacking in resources, either for staying or for leaving it").

While El Inca does not comment upon the versions of the other three de Soto chroniclers, he acknowledges the contrast in tone between his description of Apalache and that of Cabeza de Vaca. Aware of the incredulity this would cause in the minds of readers who had been exposed to *Naufragios,* El Inca takes on the issue. In Chapter IV of Book II, Part II of *La Florida,* he describes an episode in which de Soto sends out three scouts to reconnoiter the land for the best route on which to proceed, and he points out that the scout who went south, Captain Juan de Añasco, encountered territory that was much the same as the territory described in *Naufragios.* He states that the scouts who went north, Tinoco and Vasconcelos, found a densely inhabited fertile region that was free of brush and easy to traverse. El Inca then informs the reader that this episode offers an explanation of the discrepancy, reinforcing his credibility while not appearing to criticize Cabeza de Vaca. El Inca goes on to say that Cabeza de Vaca probably visited one of the minor Amerindian towns in the province of Apalache and assumed, incorrectly, that it was the principal town. His credibility is preserved at the same time a view of La Florida is presented that is likely to entice his Spanish readers to want to settle there. El Inca then offers the reader another possible reason the descriptions are different: the natives, in their eagerness to be rid of Narváez and his expedition, speak negatively of their land in order to discourage the Spanish from lingering there (198–99).

Only an individual like El Inca, whose mother's family had experienced what happened to an indigenous people whose homeland was coveted by European invaders, would think to view this situation from such a perspective. We can also see evidence within the text of *Naufragios* of how the Indians were inclined to give the Spaniards false information to entice them to leave their land and explore another region. In his Chapter IV, Cabeza de Vaca describes the scene in which the Narváez expedition arrives in La Florida. The bay-area Indians, eager to rid themselves and their territories of the Europeans, entice them to move on with false tales about gold in Apalache: "[S]eñaláronnos que muy lejos de allí había una provincia que se decía Apalache, la cual había mucho oro, y hacían seña de haber muy gran cantidad de todo lo que estimamos en algo" (87) ("They communicated to us through sign language that very far from there was a province called Apalache, where there was much gold and, they further indicated, a huge quantity of everything we esteemed").

By the time the Spaniards arrived in Apalache, their food supply had been exhausted and their interest was no longer gold. The local Indians, not wanting the soldiers to proceed any farther into their province, led them to believe that there were no food supplies in their province, probably hoping, as the Inca people had observed, that the Spaniards would return to the sea and sail away.

In summing up the differences between Cabeza de Vaca's writings and El Inca's writings, it becomes apparent that each writer wants to present La Florida to suit his own ends. A positive presentation supports El Inca's wish to promote peaceful colonization, with its accompanying conversion to Christianity of the inhabitants, while Cabeza de Vaca's objectives are served by a negative presentation. He wants the areas to appear impassible and inhospitable to support his claims to suffering, which he hopes will convince the Spanish authorities that he deserves a pension for his heroic service to the Crown in the New World.

An interesting example of El Inca's preoccupation with the commercial potential of La Florida can be seen in his descriptions of the fauna. He places special emphasis upon the marten because of the potential value of these skins on the European market. When El Inca describes how the de Soto expedition is received by the people of the chiefdom of Cofaqui, he relates that the leader, known to the Spanish as Patofa and ruling for the aging chief, or *curaca*, promises to enlist the help of the Spanish contingent to attack the people of the neighboring Cofachiqui region. According to El Inca, the *curaca* is so pleased by the prospect of destroying his hated neighbors that he gives Patofa his cape. El Inca points out to the reader that the cape is made of marten skin and emphasizes its monetary value, saying that in Spain it would be worth two thousand ducats (269–70).

Ever cognizant of the public-relations aspect of his writing, El Inca even suggests the possibility that, although de Soto and his men found almost no gold on their expedition, gold and silver may yet be found in the region: "[B]uscándolas se hallarán minas de plata y oro, como cada día en México y en el Perú se descubren de nuevo" (448) ("If a search should be made, mines of gold and silver would be found, just as new ones are discovered every day in Mexico and Peru"; 423).

In his emphasis on commercialism, El Inca exaggerates the possibility of mineral wealth in the region. He also devotes several passages to laborious descriptions of the freshwater pearls found in the area (312, 315–16). We can assume that these descriptions, like his descriptions of the flora and fauna, are exaggerated because, while Elvas and Biedma note the presence of the pearls, they do not devote as much attention to them as El Inca and they say that the pearls are not of good quality. Since Elvas, Biedma, and Rangel orient their writings toward militaristic plunder, it should be assumed that if the pearls had been of good value, they would have thought this worth including in their narratives.

El Inca's enthusiasm for the economic value of La Florida rises to a level at which the reader perceives a tone of desperation, with the author almost begging the reader to believe in the economic value of the region. He refers later in the text to the pearls, saying that the quantity to be found in the region is "increíble" (520) ("incredible"; 553). He reminds us again of the martens and goes so far as to say that the region could prove to be even more profitable than New Spain or Peru.

El Inca seems to be making the case in *La Florida* for establishing a system of *encomiendas*. El Inca believes New World natives are better protected by living and working on the large land grants than they are living independently in a Spanish-dominated society. He seems to be supporting his persuasion by engaging in what Julio Ortega refers to as "the discourse of abundance" (3). Ortega uses the phrase in reference to the *Comentarios reales,* but it is applicable to *La Florida del Inca* as well:

> El Inca Garcilaso . . . depicts the Peru of the Incas and the Peru of the Spanish empire in the language of the *conquistadores*. Himself a *mestizo*, a cultural hybrid, El Inca uses the twin concepts of hybridization and fecundity as metaphors for the fertility of the New World. After listing native fruits and plants, El Inca talks about products acclimated to Peru. (3)

One can see the precursors of this discourse of abundance in the descriptions of *La Florida*. As in the *Comentarios,* El Inca highlights the native fruits and vegetables at the same time he emphasizes the adaptability of Spanish crops to the region. In this way, he shows how the new land is similar to the native country of his readers, while maintaining very distinct differences between the two regions. He is engaging in a language of hybridization, a discourse of (agri)cultural blending. In *La Florida,* El Inca notes that the fruits of the region are "like those of Spain," but the reader can infer from his description that there are differences because he does not say that they are exactly the same. Ortega notes the same similarity/difference dichotomy in El Inca's writing: "Here we see an example of how the discourse of abundance transforms similarity . . . into an eloquent difference" (3). In one passage, El Inca points out that *calabazas* (calabashes), found in Apalache, exist also in Peru and the natives call them *zapallu* (253). In this way he not only emphasizes the difference between Europe and the New World, but he also emphasizes the similarities among the Native Americans. As part of the discourse of abundance, El Inca employs a Renaissance rhetorical device known as *locus amoenus*. In a recent study of early colonial texts in Brazil, Janiga-Perkins makes the following observation:

> Caminha presents the things and people of the New World . . . Perhaps the most striking feature . . . is the discourse of abundance, the apparent freshness, fertility, and plenty in the New World. . . . The underlying element is that none of these items has ever before been seen and recorded by Europeans. . . . *descriptio* uses European *topoi* to affix the observations of New World reality in writing, thereby lending particular meaning and importance to the object being described . . . The most frequent and persuasive commonplaces in the *Carta* are the *locus amoenus* and praise of the New World as earthly paradise. The main tenet of *locus amoenus* . . . is the exaltation of New World nature . . . Throughout the passages . . . we detect the melodious songs of the birds, the pleasing aroma of the flowers and vegetation, the healthful climate, abundant water, and idealized landscape. The *locus amoenus* greatly contributes to reader understanding of the Portuguese New World as the location of the earthly paradise . . . In Caminha's work, then, *descriptio* has firmly installed the colony into the European imaginary model of a mercantile boom waiting to happen. (18–20)

One could easily make the same observation about *La Florida*. El Inca wants the reader to view La Florida as the ideal place (*locus amoenus*) to which to relocate in pursuit of wealth and happiness. El Inca's La Florida, like Caminha's Brazil, is a boom in the making.

El Inca provides another incentive for his Catholic readers to go to La Florida by appealing to their spiritual, as well as their temporal, worldview. By pointing out that the natives cultivate the soil, he emphasizes that, even though the Indians are pagan, they have achieved a level of civilization comparable to that of the Europeans; consequently, the natives are redeemable and they will readily accept the "true faith" (Catholicism). By using this language, El Inca is subtly encouraging the effort to convert the natives in La Florida.

Where El Inca's perspective is less militaristic and is oriented toward presenting the region's potential to support agriculture and Spanish colonization, Elvas and the other chroniclers present a strictly European perspective and seem to be more concerned with explaining how the abundance of the region could support the military goals of the expedition. Elvas, Biedma, and Rangel all acknowledge the natural abundance in the region, but their descriptions are brief. They give no allusions to the potential value of the area as a place to establish *encomiendas*. Their writings do not benefit from the unique perspective of the mestizo. Elvas states:

> On Sunday, October 25, he arrived at a town called Uzela, and on Monday, at Anhaica Apalache where the lord of all that land and province lived. In that town, the *maestre de campo*, whose office is to allot and provide lodgings, lodged them all. Within a league and a half league about that town were other towns where there was an abundance of maize, pumpkins, beans, and dried plums native to the land, which are better than those of Spain and grow wild in the fields without being planted. Food which seemed sufficient to last over the winter was gathered together from those towns on into Anhaica Apalache. (71–72)

Biedma is even more brief in his description of the region and, like the author of the Elvas narrative, sees the abundance of the region only in terms of its support to the expedition:

> We crossed another river, which was in a province called Veachile, and we found some towns on the other bank, all abandoned, although we did not fail to find in them what we had need of, which was some food. We departed from here to another town, which is called Aguile. This [town] borders on that province of Apalache; a river divides the one province from the other . . . In this province of Apalache there are many towns, and it is a land of plentiful food; they call all this other land that we traveled through the province of Yustaga. (226–27)

Rangel is more militaristic in his account. He refers to the food found in Apalache as "supplies," and, as with Biedma and Elvas, his description is more brief than that of El Inca:

> The province of Apalache is very fertile and very abundant in supplies, with much corn and beans [*fésoles*] and squash [*calabazas*], and diverse fruits, and many deer and many varieties of birds, and near the sea there are many and good fish, and it is a pleasant land although there are swamps; but they are firm because they are over sand. (268)

Not only does Rangel refer to the flora and fauna of the region as "supplies," but also he writes about the region's topography as being suitable to support the logistical objectives required by de Soto and his army when he notes that the swamps were suitable to march across.

We can see El Inca's purpose of promoting colonization in La Florida and creating a positive image of the natives in another episode that he describes in a way that is strikingly different from the descriptions of his fellow chroniclers. In describing de Soto's visit to the Indian province of Coca (which probably was located in today's northeast Alabama and/or northwest Georgia), El Inca reports that the chief offers part of his province to the Spanish for settlement out of esteem and affection for de Soto. The other three give no indication of any such offer. They depict both the *cacique* (chief) and his people as duplicitous individuals who, upon the arrival of the Spanish, abandon their towns, hide in the woods, and refuse to cooperate with de Soto until he imprisons their chief and threatens them. El Inca concludes his description of this episode by saying that two individuals from de Soto's expedition remain with the Indians of Coca, and he seeks to promote more exploration and possible colonization of La Florida by provoking the curiosity of his readers: "Hicimos caudal de estas menudencias para dar cuenta de ellas para que, cuando Dios Nuestro Señor sea servido que aquella tierra se conquiste y gane, se advierta a ver si quedó algún rastro o memoria de los que así se quedaron entre los naturales de este gran reino" (395) ("We have included an account of these details so that when God, our Lord, shall will that that country be conquered and won, an effort may be made to see whether some trace or memory remains of those who thus stayed among the natives of that great kingdom"; 326).

Since El Inca claims to be concerned with the accuracy of his history, one might wonder why his version differs so significantly from those of his contemporaries. Henige notes that one must consider *La Florida* and its author in the context of their times. At the time El Inca was writing, the popular literary style for expository prose was to follow the model of the classical rhetoricians. El Inca had read extensively the classical works of Quintilian, Aristotle, Cicero, and other classical writers who considered one's argument to be more important than the truth in what one was arguing. Their tactic was to use language rather than evidence to convince the readers they were writing the truth. As a classical scholar, it was more important to El Inca to convince his reader of his accuracy than to be accurate. To this end, he utilizes the literary devices of the classical rhetoricians he had studied. The obvious progressive steps used in classical humanist rhetoric start with the obligatory expression of self-doubt and unworthiness by the author in an expression of exaggerated modesty. Henige refers to this as "tactical self-effacement" (157). Second, the author would describe an event or an object that was so extraordinary, so unbelievable that it could not be made up and, therefore, had to be true. Next, the author repeatedly assures the reader that he is speaking the truth. To accomplish this, the author repeatedly cites great authorities as the sources of his work. Henige suggests that although classical humanist rhetoricians used other tools, these are the three that are evident in El Inca's writings.

According to Henige, the goal is to write convincing rhetoric while trying to give the impression that convincing the reader is not the goal. We can see evidence of this in the passage mentioned above in which El Inca employs a self-deprecating style at the same time he attempts to convince his readers of the unreliability of the description of Apalache offered by his fellow chronicler, Cabeza de Vaca. His tone is humble, but he arrogantly asserts that his second-hand description is more reliable than the firsthand account of someone who had actually visited the region. This hyperbolized modesty is evident also in the prologue to *La Florida* when El Inca states that his primary motivation for writing *La Florida* is to help spread the Catholic faith and that he expects no "mercedes temporales" (249) ("temporal benefits"; 57) from his work. An excellent example of a description of something too extraordinary for words is seen when El Inca describes the grandeur of the dwelling place of the nobles of the province of Cofachiqui. He apologizes to his readers because he cannot find the words to describe the grand abode and its temple, and he asks that they use their imagination to supply the description because no written description would do it justice. He concludes with another assertion of veracity: "De donde . . . suplicaré encarecidamente se crea de veras que antes quedo corto y menoscabado de lo que convenía decirse que largo y sobrado en lo que se hubiere dicho" (381) ("Thus . . . I shall beg earnestly that it be believed that what has been said is an incomplete and fragmentary account, rather than an exaggerated one"; 298). In this passage we can see that El Inca directly confronts the disbelief of his readers, challenging them to believe what he has written and implying that if they do not believe it, they are not intelligent and "discretos" (381) ("judicious"; 298). Once again employing the rhetorical tactic of hyperbolized modesty, he implies that if the readers do not believe his description, not only are they exercising poor judgment, but they are also rejecting the author's sincerity.

With regard to the device of appealing to authority, Henige points out: "Elsewhere I have noted how the appeal to authority, especially the recourse to otherwise unavailable authority, is the very hallmark of the pseudo-historical output in the period immediately preceding the publication of *La Florida*" (158). The text offers numerous examples of this, particularly the prologue, in which El Inca makes repeated references to the authority of his sources, especially Gonzalo Silvestre (the old *caballero*). In one passage, he points out that not only is his source knowledgeable but he is also exceedingly trustworthy, having appeared many times before the Council of the Indies to testify about matters regarding the colonies. Aside from his judicious testimony, according to El Inca, the very fact that he is an "hombre noble" (247) ("nobleman"; 54) ensures that he is truthful at all times.

Apparently, when Renaissance writers, such as El Inca, wanted to increase interest by wild exaggeration, they tried to convince readers that anything that was unbelievable in the extreme, by its very unbelievability, had to be true; thus, the unbelievability in essence proved truthfulness. Never could an author think up the unbelievable on his own initiative; therefore, the unbelievable subject about which he was writing had to be real. The result of this rhetorical tactic is the unbelievable idealization of La Florida, which presents an image of the territory that is so often contradictory to the image presented by others. Perhaps El Inca knows that, since La Florida is virtually devoid of the precious metals the Spanish covet, it will be a hard sell to convince the Spanish government that the territory is worth colonizing, and thus he resorts to the classical tactic of super-hyperbole.

This idealization can be considered a result of El Inca's classical studies and a result of his status as a mestizo. As noted above, he is trying to create an understanding in the mind of the European reader of the new hybridized culture that is in the process of creation in the New World. This concept of mixing of cultures and ethnicities is something that is almost incomprehensible to a European of the sixteenth century who has never visited the colonial world.

El Inca is trying to create a new discourse that is capable of adequately describing the hybridizing process: a discourse of plurality, embodied by El Inca himself. Ortega notes that he is aware of the problem of believability and seeks to address it through the type of discourse noted above:

> This problem . . . is clearly of importance to El Inca, both because he is a *mestizo* living in Spain and because he aspires to rewrite history. To accomplish this, he proposes an alternative model for the verbal representation of the New World. . . . His product . . . will be a *summa*, a place for all final statements . . . about the Indians and the Spaniards, about the languages, cultures, and objects of the Old and New Worlds. It is also the theater of action for a new protagonist of plurality, the *mestizo,* a theater derived from writing and reading. (4)

I would argue that the "alternative model" presented in *La Florida del Inca* is that of idealizing the region and its inhabitants and praising the Native Americans on a level that is almost equal to the level on which he praises the Spaniards. El Inca uses the nomenclature of Spanish nobility to describe certain Native Americans as "nobles y caballeros" (274) ("nobles and *caballeros*"; 102). El Inca describes the chief Mococo in a manner that is uncharacteristic of the chroniclers of his day, but entirely consistent with his own mestizo discourse, when he points out Mococo's benevolence toward a Narváez expedition participant, Juan Ortiz.

Ortiz sought refuge with Mococo after escaping the province of a neighboring chief whose nose had been cut off by Narváez. Nose and limb severing was a common Spanish practice used to punish or gain information from Amerindians. The unfortunate chief managed to capture Ortiz and exerted revenge upon him every time he had occasion to recall the conspicuous absence of his olfactory organ. Ortiz, through the help of one of the chief's daughters, managed to escape to the safety of Mococo's province.

El Inca asserts that the behavior of Mococo far exceeds that of certain European aristocrats to whom he alludes but whom he does not name for fear of retribution (110). This statement illustrates El Inca's awareness of the limitations imposed upon him by the church and the state in Spain. He knows there are limitations on how positively he can portray Native Americans, and he is careful to avoid nonconformity to this expectation. Henige writes: "As Dowling points out, he did this by praising the Indians, on the one hand, only to surpass it with his praise of the Spanish (and Portuguese). In this sense, there are no losers in *La Florida*" (160). El Inca's Amerindian relatives assuredly practiced the same Inca custom of relating only the positive that El Inca practiced, so one can expect a compounding effect relative to all that is noble and good being incorporated into Inca history, which carried over into El Inca's compulsion to present the North American native in the same way.

In his *La Florida del Inca,* El Inca seems immersed in this contrast and contradiction. His narrative highlights the subtle contradictions present in the conquest—the religious purpose juxtaposed against the ever-present lust for gold. He narrates the exploration of lands of great natural abundance as well as of malaria-infested swamps where it would be impossible for Europeans to survive. He describes with great empathy the periods of extreme hunger and thirst de Soto and his men often endured. He writes about the contradictory relationship between the American natives and the Europeans, which so often began with friendship and hospitality and ended with conflicts that proved ruinous to both groups.

Hernández observes that the style and themes used by El Inca have a great deal to do with the "complexities and contradictions of the *mestizo* condition in those days: a complicated mixture of conflicting forces and powerful emotions" (318). He most certainly depicts La Florida in a most singular and idealized way, complete with Renaissance humanist rhetoric, Inca rhetorical traditions, classical allusions and imagery, and evangelistic zeal. His eagerness to equalize the Indians with the Spaniards is caused by his self-identification. One can imagine that his mestizo heritage gives him a self-image that is the same concept that he attaches to the North American natives. As a blood relative to the Amerindians, he seeks on their behalf the same as he seeks for himself.

Their struggles are his struggles: to find self-identity and to acquire their place in the New World social order, just as he seeks to gain his own acceptance and identity. What is their place in the race-based hierarchies of the colonial world? El Inca is attempting to devise an answer. The issue of ethnic interaction is the key to understanding the way in which El Inca chooses to approach his subject.

3
El Inca's Native Americans

Passing years and geographical space create a separation between El Inca and Peru that is permanent by the time El Inca begins to write *La Florida*. Saddened and embittered by the rejection he receives from the Spanish society into which he had hoped to be accepted, he finds his Native American identity to be a source of solace. His emotional ties to the Peruvian Amerindian culture to which his mother belonged begin to strengthen and grow. He begins to express a kinship with Native Americans throughout the Americas and to seek justice and equality on their behalf. In *La Florida del Inca*, he begins a race with time to change the perception that the natives of La Florida are barbarous and uncivilized and to see that their redeeming qualities, human potential, and noble character are included in the historical record.

El Inca's views are quite extraordinary in sixteenth-century Europe. We must remember that only half a century before *La Florida* was published, King Charles V of Spain convened a royal council of inquiry to determine whether the New World inhabitants were fully human, with the same rights as all other humans. We know from the historical record that the reality of the relationship between Spain and its colonies was one of total exploitation, with the king and his ministers demanding the New World resources while requiring that the colonists purchase all necessities from Spain. In this pecking order, Amerindians were excluded and were used as slave labor, the very worst exploitation. From the time of Columbus, the Spaniards had considered the Amerindians subhuman. El Inca is attempting to provide a counterargument to a popular conception that is one-hundred-percent negative and, with his universalist philosophy, to persuade the Spanish government and its people to respect the New World natives. Castanien states that El Inca's goal is to present the Indians in a favorable light, to counteract the idea of a barbaric people incapable of human behavior. Garcilaso takes pains to show that basically the Indians behave in much the same way as their Spanish visitors did. When it becomes necessary for him to report Indian cruelty, treachery, or other unpleasant manifestations of the human spirit, he does so, but balances such reports with incidents that show Spaniards capable of similar acts. (9)

Brading calls *La Florida del Inca* "the opening shot in Garcilaso's literary battle to rehabilitate the good name of the American Indian" (257). Continuing, Brading states, "he concentrated his energies on literary composition, seeking thus to win a name in the world of letters so as to redeem his failure to obtain recognition at court and on campaign" (256).

El Inca points out that the popular image of North American natives as heathen killers is created, at least in part, by their reaction to the rough treatment they receive at the hands of Spanish explorers:

Después, el año de mil y quinientos y cuarenta y nueve, fueron a la Florida cinco frailes de la religión de Santo Domingo. Hízoles la costa el emperador Carlos Quinto, rey de España, porque se ofrecieron a ir a predicar a aquellos gentiles el evangelio sin llevar gente de guerra, sino ellos solos, por no escandalizar aquellos bárbaros. Más ellos, que lo estaban ya de las jornadas pasadas, no quisieron oír la doctrina de los religiosos, antes, luego que los tres de ellos saltaron a la tierra, los mataron con rabia y crueldad. (522)

After 1549, five friars of the order of St. Dominic went to La Florida. The emperor Charles V, king of Spain, sent them at his expense because they offered to go and preach the gospel to those heathen without taking soldiers with them, going alone in order not to alarm those barbarians. But the latter were still disturbed from the past expeditions, and would not listen to the religious teachings. On the contrary, as soon as three of them set foot on the shore, they killed them with rage and cruelty. (556)

That El Inca is the first intellectual to recognize and protest the destructive power of globalization and the cultural hegemony it causes is a plausible argument. He believes that native cultural integrity should be respected and allowed to continue, with one exception—religion. He very sincerely wants to see the Amerindians accept the Catholic religion, but he wants the Europeans to allow native government, cultural organization, and lifestyles to continue. He knows the native Inca society very well, with its intelligent governmental organization based upon numerical sequencing relative to population numbers, labor utilization, proportional resource sharing, and multiple hierarchies of administration. El Inca's knowledge about his Peruvian ancestors and the ways in which they lived gives him the perspective that Native American culture is inextricably linked to its natural surroundings and that protecting both is vital to the Amerindians' survival. He is aware that saving the Native American culture rests upon persuasion and that persuasion rests upon astute and appropriate rhetoric in contemporary discourse. Through his writings, he hopes to convince Europeans to include native cultural integrity in their discourse and thereby ensure its continuance. El Inca realizes that cultural integrity equals cultural survival five hundred years before other scholars realize it.

The renowned linguist and postcolonial scholar Mary Louise Pratt believes that El Inca recognizes "cultura como supervivencia" (39) ("culture as survival"). She states:

> Los occidentales han tendido a funcionar con la idea de que la cultura es lo que se desarrolla una vez que un grupo tiene asegurada la subsistencia, y se define como todo aquello que existe más allá y por encima de la "mera supervivencia." Para los pueblos indígenas . . . la cultura . . . forma parte esencial de lo que está en juego en la supervivencia. La cultura es la supervivencia y por consiguiente no puede calificarse de "mera." (39)

> Westerners have tended to believe that culture is that which is developed once a group has assured its subsistence, and it is defined as all that which is over and above "mere survival." For indigenous peoples . . . culture . . . forms an essential part of survival. Culture is survival; therefore, one cannot classify it as "mere."

Pratt highlights the problem of identity encountered by El Inca and the peoples of the New World when she points out that such problems are most intense in the "zonas de contacto" (40) (zones of contact) between distinctive cultures. She states:

> En las zonas de contacto coloniales, desde una perspectiva indígena, ser "el otro" frente a una cultura dominante supone vivir en un universo bifurcado de significación. Por una parte, es necesario definirse como entidad propia para sí mismo, eso es la supervivencia. Al mismo tiempo, el sistema también exige que uno sea "el otro" para el colonizador. Nos encontramos ante un proceso que lleva produciéndose en las Américas desde

hace mucho tiempo: ese universo bifurcado en el que "el otro" tiene que sacar de sí su propio "Yo" y también "el Otro." (40)

In the colonial zones of contact, from the indigenous perspective, to be "the other" when faced with a dominant culture supposes living in a universe of bifurcated meaning. It is necessary to define oneself as one's own entity; that is survival. At the same time, the system also demands that one must be "the other" for the colonizer. We find ourselves faced with a process that has been at work in the Americas for a long time: that bifurcated universe in which "the other" has to draw from himself his own "I" and "the Other."

El Inca tries to establish this sense of "Yo" (I) for the indigenous peoples he describes and, in the process, create the same sense of identity for himself. Separated from his mother's native culture and marginalized by his paternal European culture, he is forced to create a space for himself with the tools he is most skilled at using—pen and paper. After failing to make a place for himself in European society through arms with his participation in the campaign against the Morisco (Spanish Arab) rebellion and his role in the Spanish Armada, he would have much more success through the peaceful means of discourse and rhetoric. Through writing, El Inca can gain the respect he seeks and in the process better the status of Native Americans in general. One can say that writing is the process by which El Inca forms his own sense of "Yo," thereby constituting his own personal identity. As one of the first mestizos, the problem of identity is something that El Inca grapples with his entire life, and writing is one way to resolve this issue.

OTHER DE SOTO CHRONICLES

El Inca, Elvas, Biedma, and Rangel all can be categorized as de Soto chroniclers. El Inca, Las Casas, Alonso de Ercilla, Juan de Castellanos, and Cabeza de Vaca can be categorized as chroniclers of indigenous Americans, as well as of Europeans. All the de Soto chroniclers except El Inca accompanied de Soto to the New World. No indigenous chronicler except Cabeza de Vaca ever visited the La Florida natives. The de Soto chroniclers, with the exception of El Inca, record what they learn through personal experience with the La Florida natives. El Inca's chronicle records what he learns through numerous conversations with the companion of Elvas, Biedma, and Rangel, Silvestre. No indigenous chronicler, with the exception of Cabeza de Vaca, has any personal knowledge concerning the La Florida natives, but these chroniclers are well acquainted with Amerindians in Mexico and South America. The de Soto chroniclers, with the exception of El Inca, place primary emphasis in their writings upon de Soto. The chroniclers of Native Americans place their primary emphasis upon the New World natives. All de Soto chroniclers, except El Inca, are unsympathetic to the natives; the chroniclers of the indigenous perspective are, without exception, sympathetic to the natives.

The subjects the authors choose to stress provide the greatest contrast when El Inca's narrative is compared with those of the other de Soto chroniclers, Elvas, Biedma, and Rangel. El Inca chooses to accentuate the positive, presenting the Amerindian perspective as well as the European perspective, while the other three present the European perspective only and choose to accentuate the Amerindian experience negatively. The European-oriented chroniclers give cursory coverage of subjects that El Inca covers broadly. The narratives of Rangel and Biedma, in contrast to El Inca's narrative, seem austere and distant, even though their authors were participants in the events they describe. Miró Quesada, the Peruvian literary scholar and critic, acknowledges that Rangel's narrative is the most accurate of the four de Soto chronicles in terms of details of events and accuracy of place names, but he points out that Rangel's style suffers from "rudeza de forma" (351) (crudeness of form). It is possibly because of this lack of literary elaboration that the other three de Soto narratives have not been the object of nearly as much attention as *La Florida* over the past four centuries. Even the version by the anonymous Gentleman of Elvas lacks the enthusiastic voice that we perceive in *La Florida*. One can assume that one possibility for the lack of detail about Native American life in the other three narratives is the inability of the authors to remember so many details so long after the fact. That does not impede El Inca, however, because his preoccupation with creating a certain image from a certain perspective causes him to fill in the gaps in the memory of his informant with details of his own creation.

Of the four de Soto chroniclers, El Inca is the only one who reaches a conclusion about the willingness of the natives to accept Catholicism. Among the accounts of Elvas, Biedma, and Rangel, none makes any suppositions about the potential for evangelization among the natives, although they do recount some of their indigenous religious practices.

All Spanish chroniclers who are sympathetic to the Native American cause write with the same restraints set upon them by European thinking, the Spanish government, and the Catholic hierarchy. The Spanish king and his government expect all writers to avoid any comments that in any way criticize the king, his policies, or his government, and the Catholic Inquisition Committee reviews all books that are to be published in Spain to ensure compliance with Catholic thinking. In spite of these constraints, El Inca and all the sympathetic chroniclers—the priest Las Casas, the soldier-poet Alonso de Ercilla, the Spanish writer Juan de Castellanos, and the explorer Cabeza de Vaca—contribute to changing European thinking about the New World natives. It is Las Casas, Ercilla, and El Inca who use civilizing rhetoric to establish the Native American image as that of the Noble Savage, which becomes standard in colonial writing. Ercilla and El Inca base their civilizing rhetoric upon classical and Renaissance writings, while Las Casas's rhetoric has a legalistic tone. El Inca is the first among the sympathetic chroniclers to observe similarities between classical civilizations and the New World natives and to use this comparison as a civilizing tool:

> His Indian warriors often act like red-skinned Europeans possessing feudal institutions . . . and they also display pride of lineage, profound class cleavage, lofty concepts of honor, and a predilection for single combat. The dusky chieftains of Florida, Georgia, and Alabama deliver long, florid speeches which sparkle with noble sentiments of honor and fidelity . . . Thus the Inca Garcilaso helped the poet, Alonso de Ercilla, and the polemical Bartolomé de las Casas to create the myth of the "noble savage" destined for later popularity in European letters. (Leonard, "The Inca," 58)

Sixteenth-century Europeans are extremely subjective thinkers, and in their subjectivity they believe no society is humanized until it is Europeanized—exhibiting values that are equal to their values. To the sixteenth-century European reader, Europeanization equals humanization. As a result of this attitude, all sympathetic Spanish chroniclers universalize, Europeanize, and civilize to humanize and legitimize the Native Americans to Europeans. Explicitly or implicitly, these authors portray the Amerindians not as mindless savages but as astute leaders similar to their European counterparts, with both noble and less-than-noble characteristics.

EL INCA COMPARED WITH OTHER CHRONICLERS

Although he acknowledges the Indians' lack of scientific sophistication, El Inca differs from the other Amerindian-sympathetic chroniclers because, while they see the natives as showing a potentiality toward becoming civilized, El Inca sees them as already possessing civilization. El Inca refers to their chiefdoms as "provinces" in an attempt to Europeanize and thereby humanize Native Americans in European public opinion. Civilizing the Amerindians to the Europeans is so vital in his reasoning that he uses greatly exaggerated rhetoric: "muchas veces me pesó hallarlas en el discurso de la historia tan políticas, tan magníficas y excelentes, porque no se sospechase que eran ficciones mías y no cosecha de al tierra" (521) ("often in the course of this History, I have been apprehensive at finding them so civilized, magnificent, and excellent, fearing that it may be suspected that these things were inventions of my own and not virtues of the country"; 553).

Taking into account El Inca's more enthusiastic style, Pastor is able to distinguish several characteristics of the chronicles that can be applied equally to El Inca and Ercilla. She observes that many conquest narratives describe the conquered lands as a "región fabulosa" (263) ("fabulous region"). As noted in Chapter 2, El Inca employs this rhetorical device in the form of his "discourse of abundance." This type of exaggeration is what Pastor calls the "modelo de representación" (397) ("model of representation"). This discourse method is the means by which Ercilla, El Inca, and other chroniclers give legitimacy to their narratives. She notes the "reivindación de la humanidad y excelencia del indígena pasa necesariamente por su integración ficticia dentro del contexto ideológico y literario occidental" ("claim of the humanity and excellence of the indigenous people arises through its fictitious integration into the Western ideological and literary context"), which gives the narratives an "estructura integradora cuya función fundamental es la *autorización* del material narrativo, de la percepción que expresa y de las propuestas que en él se inscriben" (391) ("integrative structure, the purpose of which is the *authorization* of the narrative material, through the perception that it expresses and its inherent ideas"). This process of legitimization serves to "autorizar y prestigiar los elementos que este paisaje tipificado enmarca" (397) ("lend authority and prestige to the elements that are characteristic of this type of description"). The "modelo" employed by El Inca, Ercilla, and other writers sympathetic to the native cause serves to convince the reader that Native Americans are civilized in the same way that pagans of classical antiquity were civilized: they have a great deal of human potential, but to achieve it, they need Christian redemption. Pastor's analysis of Ercilla's *La Araucana* could just as easily be applied to *La Florida*:

> La enumeración casi exhaustiva de los elementos que componen el modelo renacentista de representación . . . cumple la misma función que la mención explícita del orden y *artificio* que califican . . . las acciones de los araucanos: definirlos como pueblo civilizado. (398)

> The exhaustive enumeration of the elements that comprise the Renaissance model of representation . . . serves the same function as the explicit mention of the order and *artifice* that characterize . . . the actions of the Araucanians: defining them as a civilized people.

One could quite easily substitute the name of almost any indigenous group from *La Florida* for "los araucanos" ("the Araucanians") and come to the same conclusion. Pastor observes that this method of representing the natives of the

New World, which she calls the "modelo renacentista" ("Renaissance model"), serves a two-part function. First, it "cancela la connotación de barbarie que se percibe en la época como inseparable de lo americano" (398) ("cancels the connotation of barbarism that is perceived during this period as inseparable from all things American"). Second, it serves to assimilate Native American civilization into the traditions of European civilizations. By associating Native American civilization with European civilization, this type of discourse gives legitimacy to a Native American past that had been largely ignored by other authors. El Inca and Ercilla seek to legitimize Amerindian traditions by making them part of the Western literary tradition (398–99). Pastor notes, however, that the goals of Ercilla and El Inca are slightly different. Ercilla seeks to ennoble the Native American through a symbolic restitution of traditional Native American society, which he achieves through his poem by inventing a history for them based on the model of classical antiquity. Although El Inca employs similar rhetorical devices, he does not want to create a fictitious history; he wants to restore and protect the true history and traditions of native peoples, and his use of Renaissance rhetorical devices, including hyperbole and embellished descriptions, serves him only as a means to achieve that goal:

> [E]s igualmente importante señalar que, frente a una serie de discursos narrativos de la conquista de América, que desde Colón hasta Ercilla, habían despojado al hombre Americano de cualquier forma de palabra, cultura e historia, en *La Araucana* se lleva a cabo una restitución simbólica de esos mismos tres elementos. El intento de recuperación auténtica del pasado indígena y su incorporación real a la historia no le corresponderá al proyecto de Ercilla sino al discurso del Inca Garcilaso, a través de lo que Pupo-Walker ha llamado con acierto la "peregrinación imaginativa hacia la historia." (402–3)

> [I]t is equally important to note that a series of narratives about the conquest of America, from Columbus to Ercilla, had depicted Native Americans as lacking any form of literature, culture, and history[;] in *La Araucana* we see a symbolic restitution of these three elements. The intent of authentic restitution of the indigenous past and its incorporation into history is not the purpose of Ercilla's work, but rather the discourse of El Inca Garcilaso, through what Pupo-Walker has called the "imaginative pilgrimage toward history."

As for Las Casas, his style is less literary than that of his contemporaries. His works are more like legal documents as he is attempting to argue for recognition of basic human rights for the Amerindians by Spain's government;

this does not make his works less relevant to the causes pursued by all the sympathetic chroniclers. Las Casas, like El Inca, recognizes that conversion of the Native Americans to Catholicism should not mean the destruction of their society. Unlike El Inca, he does not recognize that the level of social development of the Native Americans balances that of the Europeans and the great civilizations of antiquity.

After El Inca, Alonso de Ercilla comes closer than the other three Amerindian-sympathetic chroniclers to Europeanizing the Native American image. In a sixteenth-century context, the chronicle is considered historically accurate, while poetry is considered entertaining; consequently, the concept of human dignity and the comparative worthiness of indigenous Americans receive greater consideration through El Inca's works than through his soldier-poet predecessor's poetry.

El Inca's ideas about the Noble Savage are closer to those in Ercilla's writing than they are to those of the other three de Soto chroniclers. One can discern similarities between their writing styles and see influences of the soldier-poet Ercilla on the narrative style of the soldier-historian, El Inca. Both Leonard and Quesada note that *La Araucana* influenced El Inca:

> [D]ebió de influir en Garcilaso el resonante poema de Alonso de Ercilla *La Araucana,* cuyas dos primeras partes se publicaron en 1569 y 1578, o sea antes de que El Inca escribiera su historia, y la tercera en 1589, o sea antes que el escritor cuzqueño la reelaborara con las informaciones de Carmona y de Coles. "Araucana en prosa" ha llamado precisamente Ventura García Calderón a *La Florida,* en una frase feliz que ha hecho fortuna. Y hay en verdad una línea común de semejanzas entre el poema histórico de Ercilla (que el propio Garcilaso juzgaba que alcanzaría mayor crédito de estar escrito en prosa) y la historia con adornos poéticos del Inca, en la que también se cantan los paisajes agrestes y las hazañas guerreras de América, y se enaltecen por igual las virtudes de "heroicos caualleros Españoles e Indios." (Quesada 350)

> [T]he influence of Ercilla's poem, *La Araucana,* resonates in the work of Garcilaso. The poem's first two parts were published in 1569 and 1578, before El Inca wrote his history, and the third part in 1589, before El Inca rewrote his work with the new information provided by Carmona and Coles. "*Araucana* in prose" is what Ventura García Calderón has called *La Florida,* with a phrase that has become commonplace. There are similarities between Ercilla's historical poem (that Garcilaso himself thought would have achieved greater credibility had it been written in prose) and the history with poetic adornment of El Inca, in which he also praises the

American countryside and heroic deeds of Americans, and he praises equally the virtues of "heroic Spanish and Indian knights."

The strong relationship between El Inca's and Ercilla's writings necessarily requires exploring Ercilla's epic poem.

As noted by Quesada, *La Araucana* was published in three parts. The epic poem is a *La Florida*–like narrative in verse, just as Calderón has suggested that *La Florida* is *La Araucana* in prose. Alonso de Ercilla, like El Inca, was both soldier and scholar. As such, he was able to compose a narrative in verse describing the sixteenth-century rebellion of the Araucanian Amerindians against the Spanish and the Spanish military campaign that put down the rebellion in the region that became Chile. Ercilla is able to give a firsthand account of these events because he participated in the campaign. Although El Inca's narrative of *La Florida* is based upon secondhand testimony, with occasional gaps of information that allow for considerable creative license, Ercilla's narrative is equally embellished, filled with lofty rhetoric and hyperbole. As we shall see, this similarity exists because, first, El Inca had read Ercilla's poem and, second, because El Inca and Ercilla studied the classics and both adapted the rhetorical style within them to their own writing.

The Italian Renaissance writers Ariosto and Boiardo revived the literary techniques used in the classical heroic epic, and this was an accepted literary style when Ercilla wrote his poem. Ercilla utilizes these literary techniques, with one exception: the predominant paradigm in the classical epic—portraying fictitious events—gives way to reality. Ercilla's epic poem and El Inca's narrative relate real, contemporary events.

Although Ercilla bases his epic poem upon reality, like El Inca he relies upon the traditions in the medieval Spanish romance to help him embellish scenes in his narrative. The battle scenes in particular, as Brading has observed, bear evidence of the influence of medieval epics like *El Cid*. Both El Inca and Ercilla try to present their narratives within the context of the inevitable diffusion of Christianity, a theme popular among the medieval epic romances. Brading notes, "Ercilla sought to dignify his epic by frequent allusion to Classical heroes and scenes, including Virgil's *Dido* and, equally important, included a lengthy narration of the Christian victory over the Turks at the Battle of Lepanto" (56). This, too, is one of El Inca's objectives.

Ercilla shows a classical antiquity style, portraying natives as "a hearty, freedom-loving nation of barbarian warriors whose state was governed by a confederacy of war-chiefs who met in 'senate' to prepare for the defense of their '*patria*' [homeland] from foreign dominion, be it of the Incas or the Spaniards" (Brading 56). El Inca does the same, but less because of classical influences, although they are present, than because of the influence of his maternal heritage and his consequential urge to elevate the status of the natives of the New World to that of equal partner in the vast enterprise that we now call the colonial experience. Both El Inca and Ercilla are establishing the Native American as a Noble Savage.

Like El Inca, Ercilla seeks to create a moral equivalency between the Native Americans and the Christians of the Iberian Peninsula. Like El Inca, Ercilla walks a fine line between exalting the Native American and arousing the anger and suspicion of the Spanish authorities, both religious and secular. Ercilla had the capacity to "recognize the justice of the Araucanian cause and the courage with which they defended their freedom, without in any way conceding the claims of the Spanish monarchy to govern the New World," at the same time he "fully acknowledged the justice of the Indian struggle to preserve their freedom, admitting that the first Spanish governor, Pedro de Valdivia, had not restrained the landowners from oppressing their native subjects" (Brading 56–57). Both authors infer that the natives of the regions about which they write might have welcomed the Gospel preaching had the Spanish not treated them so cruelly. El Inca stresses that the Native Americans will not be willing to listen to and accept Christianity unless Europeans treat them equitably.

While acknowledging that the natives are in need of Christian redemption, Ercilla emphasizes their strength and character, thereby emphasizing the strength and character of those who defeat them: the Spanish. Although the Amerindians of *La Araucana* are misguided in their pagan ways, their cause is just.

Like Ercilla, El Inca attempts to rationalize some of the cruel behavior of the natives. For example, the cacique Hirrihigua, who abused Juan Ortiz, the survivor of the ill-fated Narváez expedition, is presented as partially justified in his actions because of the abuse the members of the expedition had heaped upon the chief while they were in La Florida. El Inca does not excuse Hirrihigua but, like Ercilla, shows the reader that the abusive nature of the colonial experience is a "two-way street." El Inca, like Ercilla, again stresses the nobility of the Native Americans. Hirrihigua's semibarbaric behavior stands in sharp contrast to the behavior of his daughters, who intercede on behalf of Ortiz on numerous occasions, convincing Hirrihigua to spare his life, and who help him escape to a neighboring province. El Inca and Ercilla imply that Spanish cruelty equals or exceeds Indian cruelties.

Whereas Ercilla critiques the cruelty he witnesses, El Inca is trying to prevent it. Both authors accomplish their purpose while striking a delicate balance between showing greater sympathy for the natives and their plight and avoiding language that would be offensive to the Spanish government. Both know the limits of the government's tolerance. Neither Ercilla nor El Inca ever questions the legitimacy of the pretensions of the monarchy to rule the New World and the people in it. Both strive to maintain a balance between a "sympathetic portrayal of native virtue" (Brading 57) and a sympathetic portrayal of the divine right of kings to rule their subjects.

Cabeza de Vaca is the chronicler who comes closest to sharing El Inca's mestizo-humanist discourse, but he learned respect and sympathy toward the Amerindians and their culture the hard way. After escaping from the hostile Indians who captured him when a shipwreck cast him upon their shores near what is today Galveston, Texas, he wandered through the wilderness toward Mexico. In this approximately ten-year encounter, a kinder and gentler Indian society gave him needed assistance. The time spent within this native culture changed his European perspective toward the Native Americans. His writings exhibit this change in his perspective. At the beginning of *Naufragios,* he describes the Indians as dishonest and barbaric. By the end of his narrative, he applies such negative adjectives to his Spanish contemporaries. In one memorable scene, he defends his native companions against Spanish slave catchers. As he describes the scene, he editorializes about the nature of the Native American–European relationship:

> Ellos no querían sino ir con nosotros hasta dejarnos, como acostumbraban, con otros indios . . . que para ir con nosotros no temían a los cristianos ni a sus lanzas. A los cristianos les pesaba de esto, y hacían que su lengua les dijese que nosotros éramos de ellos mismos . . . y que ellos eran los señores de aquella tierra, a quien habían de obedecer y servir. Más todo esto los indios . . . entre sí platicaban, diciendo que los cristianos mentían, porque nosotros veníamos de donde salía el Sol, y ellos donde se pone. Que nosotros sanábamos los enfermos y ellos mataban los que estaban sanos; y que nosotros veníamos desnudos y descalzos, y ellos . . . con lanzas. Que nosotros no teníamos codicia de ninguna cosa, antes todo cuanto nos daban tornábamos luego a dar, y con nada nos quedábamos, y los otros no tenían otro fin sino robar todo cuanto hallaban, y nunca daban nada a nadie. (205)

> They [the natives] wanted only to accompany us until they had handed us over to other Indians, as was their custom. . . . they did not fear the Christians [Spanish slave catchers] or their lances when they were with us. The Christians did not like this and had their interpreter tell them that we were the same kind of people they [the other Spaniards] were . . . They said that they were the lords of that land, and that the Indians should obey and serve them, but the Indians believed very little or nothing of what they were saying. Speaking among themselves, they said instead that the Christians were lying because we had come from the East

and they [the slavers] had come from the West; that we healed the sick and they killed the healthy; that we were naked and barefooted and they were dressed and . . . with lances; that we coveted nothing but instead gave away everything that was given to us and kept none of it, while the sole purpose of the others was to steal everything they found, never giving anything to anybody.

El Inca's mestizo-humanist discourse, however, provides an interpretation that his contemporaries could not employ. Even those, like Cabeza de Vaca, who shared his intentions toward the Amerindians, were not mestizos and consequently could not share his discourse. We can see that Cabeza de Vaca, through his isolated experience with the Indians, has become "the other." In contrast, El Inca, being born a mestizo, is "the other," which gives him insights that no one born in Europe, not even de Vaca, can possess.

El Inca, through his mestizo-humanist discourse in *La Florida,* provides us with one of the first reliable sources of information about the natives of North America. In this regard, it is more than just a chronicle, it is an anthropological exposition. Although not an eyewitness, having never visited North America, El Inca gives a vision of the North American natives that is vivid, although idealized, to the point that we see them as real, living human beings.

EL INCA'S LITERARY TECHNIQUE

In *La Florida,* El Inca is happy to record what accurate history he is able to obtain concerning the Native Americans, but his informant's memory cannot give him all that he needs. When his narrative requires content not available to him, he applies all the techniques in Renaissance and classical writings that change weak presentations into strong ones to help him present the Indians as he longs to have them perceived—in some aspects with less civility than the Europeans, in other aspects with greater civility, and, when all comparisons are complete, possessing a character that, in the aggregate, is as noble and honest as that possessed by Europeans. Throughout his narrative, El Inca implicitly and at times explicitly conveys this perception to his readers. Religion is the one area in which El Inca states the Native Americans are not as noble as the Europeans, but he believes that they will accept Christianity willingly and that in religion, also, they will become as noble.

Even while proposing that the La Florida natives need to accept Christianity and end their pagan practices, El Inca continues his theme of civilizing discourse. El Inca's view that the Amerindians in La Florida would accept Christianity were they given the chance is a radical departure from the popular theological view held by many of his contemporaries that Christ traveled to the

New World after the resurrection and witnessed to the Amerindians, only to see them reject his teachings (José Rabasa). As a Catholic and a mestizo, El Inca holds no such belief, as is evident in his writings.

El Inca is trying to convey to his European readers that the La Florida natives are more inclined to accept Christianity because paganism as they practice it gives them a heightened state of religious consciousness. They were regarded by some of Spain's religious leaders as less prone to the worship of idols than other natives of the New World. El Inca emphasizes this when he points out that although the La Florida inhabitants have pagan temples and worship the sun and the moon, they worship without idols or human sacrifice (68).

THE NATIVE LIFESTYLE

El Inca gives his perspectives, written with great generosity, about the Amerindians' buildings, towns, natural resources, clothes, jewelry, physical appearance, strength, skills and expertise in war, possessions, living habits, diet, and other subjects. He writes objectively about the deeds of the natives, but, more important, he also gives us an idea of their emotions and motivations.

The natives' diet is of particular interest to El Inca. After introducing Hernando de Soto, listing others who had visited Florida, and talking about the Indians' general living habits, he approaches this subject. Elvas, without comment or elaboration, states that the Indians' diet consists primarily of maize, squash, and wild game. El Inca, in contrast, names what they eat and how they prepare it:

[E]l comer ordinario de ellos es el maíz en lugar de pan, y por vianda frisoles y calabaza de las que acá llaman romana, y mucho pescado, conforme a los ríos de que gozan. De carne tienen carnestía, porque no la hay de ninguna suerte de ganado manso. Con los arcos y flechas matan mucha caza de ciervos, corzos y gamos, que los hay mucho en número y más crecidos que los de España. . . . Su bebida es agua clara, como la dio la naturaleza, sin mezcla de cosa alguna. La carne y pescado que comen ha de ser muy asado o muy cocido, y la fruta muy madura, y en ninguna manera la comen verde ni a medio madurar, y hacían burla de que los castellanos comiesen agraz. (255–56)

[T]heir ordinary food is maize, in place of bread, and their viands are beans and calabashes of the variety they call here *romana,* and a great deal of fish because of the many rivers they possess. There is a scarcity of meat, for they have no species of domesticated cattle. They kill in the chase with their bows and arrows red deer, fallow deer, and roe deer, which are numerous and larger than those of Spain. . . . Their drink is clear water, just as nature gives it to them, without the admixture of anything else. The meat and the fish they eat must be very well dressed and cooked, and the fruit very ripe. They will never eat it green or half-ripe and laugh at the Castilians for eating green fruit. (69)

Using the discourse of abundance that appears throughout the book, El Inca points out that the deer of La Florida are larger than their Spanish counterparts and that the many rivers of the region offer fish in abundance (69).

El Inca relates also how the natives' knowledge about a salt substitute healed the Spanish soldiers and literally saved the army: "luego que nuestros españoles salieron de la gran provincia de Coza y entraron en la Tascaluza, tuvieron necesidad de sal, habiendo pasado algunos días sin ella, la sintieron de manera que les hacía mucha falta . . . pora falta . . . extrañísima" (428) ("as soon as our Spaniards left the great province of Coca [Coosa] and entered that of Tascalusa they were in need of salt. Having passed some days without it, they felt the lack of it greatly . . . and the need of it in a most extraordinary manner"; 383–84). El Inca states that the Spanish exhibited some very strange symptoms and "perecían sin remedio alguno" (428) ("they perished without any help for it"; 384). In this instance, the Amerindians' knowledge surpassed what the Spaniards knew. The natives had a remedy that, when applied early enough, could save them: "quemaban cierta yierba que ellos conocían y de la ceniza hacían lejía, y en ella, como en salsa, mojaban lo que comían" (428) ("they burned a certain herb they knew about and made lye with the ashes. They dipped what they ate into it as if it were a sauce"; 384). Some Spaniards used the remedy; others "por ser soberbios y presuntuosos no querían usar de este remedio por parecerles cosa sucia" (428) ("in their arrogance and presumptuousness were unwilling to make use of this remedy because they regarded it as a filthy thing"; 384). They were without salt almost a year, and in this time over sixty Spaniards perished. El Inca then says, "y en su lugar diremos cómo hicieron sal y socorrieron su necesidad" (428) ("and we shall tell in due time how they made salt and supplied their need"; 384). El Inca explains:

[L]legaron a la ribera de un río . . . Ciertos soldados, después de haber hecho su alojamiento, se bajaron paseando al río y, andando por la orilla, echaron de ver en una arena azul, que había a la lengua del agua, uno de ellos, tomando de ella, la gustó, y halló que era salobre, y dio aviso a los compañeros y les dijo que le parecía se podría hacer salitre de aquella arena para hacer pólvora para los arcabuces. Con esta intención dieron en la coger mañosamente, procurando coger la arena azul sin mezcla de la blanca. Habiendo cogido alguna cantidad, la echaron en agua y en ella la estregaron entre las manos, y colaron el agua, y la pusieron a cocer, la cual, con el mucho fuego que le dieron, se convirtió en sal algo amarilla de color, más de gusto y de afecto de salar muy buena. Con el regocijo de la nueva invención, y por la mucha necesidad que tenían de sal, pararon los españoles ocho días en aquel alojamiento, y hicieron gran cantidad de ella. Algunos hubo que, con el ansia que tenían de sal, viéndose ahora con abundancia de ella, la comían a bocados sola, como si fuera azúcar, y a los que se lo reprehendían les decían: "Dejadnos hartar de sal, que harta hambre hemos traído de ella." Y de tal manera se hartaron nueve o diez de ellos, que en pocos días murieron de hidropesía, porque a unos mata la hambre y a otros el hastío. (442)

[T]hey came to the bank of a river . . . certain soldiers went down to walk by the river, [and] in passing along the shore they happened to see a blue sand at the water's edge. One of them took up some of it, tasted it, and found that it was brackish. He told his companions, and they said that they thought saltpeter could be made of it for making powder for the *harquebuses*. With this in mind they set to work handily to take up the blue sand without an admixture of the white. Having collected a quantity of it, they put it in the water, rubbed it together between their hands, strained off the water, and put it to boil. As they made a large fire under it, it was converted into salt of a somewhat yellow color, but effective and with a very good taste. Rejoicing at this new discovery, and because of the great need for salt, the Spaniards spent eight days in that camp and made a large quantity of it. There were some who in their craving for salt, seeing that there was now an abundance of it, ate it by itself in mouthfuls, as if it were sugar. To those who scolded them they said, "Let us get our fill of salt, because we have had a great craving for it." Nine or ten of them ate their fill of it in such a manner that in a few days they died of dropsy. Thus some died from lack of salt and some from too much. (410)

Immediately after the description of the native diet, El Inca continues with a citation of one of his fellow chroniclers that is intended to debunk a persistent rumor about the people in the New World. El Inca's preoccupation with improving the Native American image in the minds of his European readers is evident once again in his statement:

Los que dicen que comen carne humana se lo levantan, a lo menos a los que son de las provincias que nuestro gobernador descubrío; antes lo abominan, coma la nota Alvar Núñez Cabeza de Vaca en sus *Naufragios*, capítulo catorce, y diez y siete, donde dice que de hambre murieron cier-

tos castellanos que estaban alojados aparte y que los compañeros que
quedaban comían los que se morían hasta el postrero, que no hubo quién
lo comiese, de lo cual dice que se escandalizaron los indios tanto que es-
tuvieron por matar todos los que habían quedado en otro alojamiento.
(256)

Those who say they eat human flesh attribute this to them falsely, at least
to those of the provinces our governor discovered. On the contrary they
abominate it, as Alvar Núñez Cabeza de Vaca notes in Chapters 14 and 17
of his *Naufragios,* where he says that certain Castilians who were lodged
apart died of hunger, and that their remaining companions ate those who
had died, except for the buttocks, which none of them would eat, where-
upon, he says, the Indians were so scandalized that they were on the point
of killing all those who were left in another lodging. (69)

El Inca continues his narration, explaining the natives' living habits. His approach to the subject matter differs from that of his contemporaries in his description of the towns and dwellings of the natives of La Florida. He diverges
from the approach of most other chroniclers of the conquest because he does
not use the natives as background for detailed descriptions of the "heroic" adventures of the Spanish explorers. This is the very thing he seeks to avoid in
his chronicle.

As El Inca describes the region of Osachile in the Florida panhandle, he
notes not just that the houses there were of wood and palm leaves but also that
the town was quite large and contained "doscientas casas grandes y buenas"
(318) ("two hundred large and good houses"; 184). The Gentleman of Elvas, in
describing the arrival of de Soto's force at the town of Ucita, not only gives a
very cursory description but also demonstrates a profound lack of knowledge
of Native American culture typical of one familiar with a European discourse
only. He states, "The town consisted of seven or eight houses. The chief's house
stood near the beach on a very high hill that had been artificially built as a
fortress. . . . The houses were of wood and were covered with palm leaves" (57).

INDIAN MOUNDS AND MISSISSIPPIAN CULTURE

The earthen mounds to which Elvas refers, common in the towns of the Mississippian Amerindian culture, were used for ceremonial purposes and to de-
note the rank of those living atop them. Elvas's misinterpretation of the purpose of the earthen mounds contributes to reinforcing the image of Native
Americans as a group of people who do not share characteristics present in
European society, such as a hierarchical social structure and religious values.

As a European, and by popular definition superior to the natives, Elvas no doubt felt that his cursory interpretation of this aspect of native culture was correct and did not merit further investigation.

El Inca's narrative, in contrast with those of his fellow chroniclers, demonstrates his preoccupation with conveying to his European readers the sense that Amerindian society is, in fact, similar to European society in this level of civilization. Similarities between the La Florida natives' walled towns, with their mounds in the center, and the medieval fortified estates common in western Europe will not escape his attention. His status as a mestizo gives him access to both European and native discourse and allows him to provide an accurate interpretation of the ceremonial mounds, as well as details about their proportions and manner of construction. His ability to interpret the significance of the mounds is enhanced when he remembers his Peruvian relatives' conversations about ancient Inca holy sites and religious ceremonies.

El Inca gives the reader what is considered by modern scholars to be a very accurate description of the construction and purpose of Mississippian ceremonial mounds. Lawrence Clayton and colleagues note that, in spite of some exaggerations, El Inca's descriptions of the Mississippian-period Indian townships that de Soto's group encountered are some of the most accurate of the colonial period (331). One such description reads:

> Para lo cual es de saber que los indios de la Florida siempre procuraron poblar en alto, siquiera las casas de los caciques y señores cuando no podían todfo el pueblo. Y porque toda la tierra es muy llana y pocas veces hallan sitio alto que tenga las demás comodidades útiles y necesarias para poblar, lo hacen a fuerza de sus brazos, que, amontonando grandísima cantidad de tierra, la ban pisando fuertemente, levantándola en forma de serro de dos y tres picas en alto, y encima hacen un llano capez de diez o doce, quince o veinte casas, para morada del señor y de su familia y gente de servicio, conforme a su posibilidad y grandeza del estado. En lo llano, al pie del cerro . . . hacen una plaza cuadrada, según tamaño de pueblo que le ha de poblar; alrededor de ella hacen los más nobles y principales sus casas, y luego la demás gente común las suyas. Procuran no alejarse del cerro donde está la casa del señor, antes trabajan de cercarle con las suyas. (319–20)

Therefore it is to be noted that the Indians of La Florida always endeavor to live on a high point, at least in the case of the houses of the *caciques* and lords when the whole pueblo cannot do so. And because the whole country is very flat, and an elevated site is seldom found that has the other conveniences useful and necessary for a settlement, they make it by their own labor. Amassing a very large quantity of earth, they pack it down by treading on it, raising it up in the form of a hill two or three pike-lengths in height. On top they make a level space large enough for ten, twelve, fifteen, or twenty houses for the dwellings of the lord and his family and the people in his service, in accordance with his ability and the grandeur of his state. On the plain at the foot of the hill . . . they make a square plaza corresponding to the size of the pueblo that is to be settled, surrounding which the nobles and chief men build their houses. Then the rest of the common people build theirs, endeavoring not to be too far from the hill where the lord's house is; they try rather to surround his with their own. (186)

Modern scholars regard this description as the most accurate of all that were given in the chronicles. Archaeologists, such as Vernon Knight in his annotations of *The Florida of the Inca* in *The De Soto Chronicles*, have affirmed its accuracy:

This remarkable passage describing general Mississippian mound construction and the ideal village layout is not duplicated in the other De Soto narratives and is the earliest on record. Moreover, its essential accuracy, except for the apparently exaggerated number of buildings claimed for the mound's summit is confirmed many times over in archeological investigations throughout the Southeast. (185 n. 9)

Once again, El Inca's interpretative accuracy puts him ahead of his time. His cogent observations concerning the mounds show his broad knowledge about Amerindians, as well as his creativity as a writer and historian. Marvin T. Smith, in his article "Indian Responses to European Contact: The Coosa Example," states that the "presence of the mounds serves as testimony of the coercive power of the chiefs to conscript labor for large construction projects. The chiefs had the power to force their subjects to perform such labor and controlled the stored food surpluses to support the workers" (135).

EUROPEANIZING THE INDIAN

El Inca also observes the dress and adornments worn by the Amerindians, pointing out that they, like Europeans, distinguish among social groups using headdresses and other adornments and that natives have a stratified hierarchical social structure similar to that in Spain. He is Europeanizing his native images to prove to his readers that La Florida natives are, in their own way, as aristocratic and as honorable as the Europeans. El Inca notes the distinction among classes in Amerindian society, an observation no doubt enhanced by his knowledge of the complex hierarchical structure of Inca society. He expands upon his observations: "Matan mucha diversidad de aves, así para comer la carne como para adornar sus cabezas con las plumas, que las tienen de diversos colores y galanas de media braza en alto, que traen sobre las cabezas, con las cuales se diferencian los nobles de los plebeyos en la paz, y los soldados de los no soldados en la guerra" (255–56) ("They kill many kinds of birds, both in order to eat the flesh and to adorn their heads with the feathers, which they wear in showy, multicolored headdresses half a fathom tall; thereby they distinguish the nobles from the plebeians in time of peace and the soldiers from those who are not such in time of war"; 69). Such an observation surely would signify to a reader from the highly stratified society of western Europe that there is order to Native American society and its members are not just a group of savage beings living in a precivilized condition.

How the Amerindians view their possessions is included in El Inca's Europeanizing discourse as well. He points out that the Indians see their possessions not in monetary terms but as having utilitarian, esthetic, emotional, religious, and sentimental value. This contrasts with Elvas's subjective viewpoint that sees the Indians' possessions in monetary terms only. The European image that New World natives are people who have no values that equal European values is reinforced by Elvas's comments in his chronicle: "Some pearls, spoiled by fire and of little value were found there. The Indians bore them through in order to string them for beads, which are worn around the neck or arm, and they esteem them greatly" (57). His evaluation of the pearls worn by the Indians as being of "little value" because they are "spoiled by fire" yet as being greatly esteemed by the Indians in their spoiled state reinforces the European image about values.

NATIVE AMERICAN PHYSICAL TRAITS

The physical characteristics of the natives of La Florida are astonishing to all the de Soto chroniclers, but it is El Inca, once again, who gives these characteristics the broadest coverage. All the colonial chroniclers—Spanish, French, and British—write about the natives' astonishing stature and strength, and all agree that the stature of the average native is greater than that of the average European. Cabeza de Vaca observes:

Hubo hombres este día que juraron que habían visto dos robles, cada uno de ellos tan grueso como la pierna por bajo pasados, de parte a parte de las flechas de los indios; y esto no es tanto de maravillar, vista la fuerza y maña con que las echan . . . Cuantos indios vimos desde La Florida aquí todos son flecheros; y como son tan crecidos de cuerpo y andan desnudos, desde lejos parecen gigantes. Es gente a maravilla bien dispuesta, muy enjutos y de muy grandes fuerzas y ligereza. Los arcos que usan son gruesos como el brazo, de once a doce palmos de largo, que flechan a doscientos pasos con tan gran tiento, que ninguna cosa yerran. (100)

There were men who swore that they had seen two oak trees, each as thick as a man's lower leg, pierced from one side to the other by Indian arrows. This is not so surprising considering the strength and skill they have when shooting. . . . All the Indians we had seen in Florida were archers, and since they were so tall, and they were naked, from a distance they looked like giants. They are quite handsome, very lean, very strong and fast. Their bows are as thick as an arm and eleven or twelve spans long. They shoot their arrows from a distance of two hundred paces with such accuracy that they never miss.

El Inca similarly describes Chief Vitachuco of the Florida panhandle: "El cual sería de edad de treinta y cinco años, de muy buena estatura de cuerpo, como generalmente lo son todos los indios de la Florida" (305) ("He was about thirty-five years of age, of very good stature, as are all the Indians of La Florida generally"; 161). Asserting that one with such good stature surely would appear gallant, El Inca continues: "mostraba bien en su aspecto la bravosidad de su ánimo" (305) ("his aspect showed clearly the gallantry of his spirit"; 161). El Inca knows that the rest of the story reveals that Vitachuco plotted to destroy de Soto and his army and that civilizing rhetoric is needed to counterbalance what this plot suggests about Vitachuco's character. El Inca states that Vitachuco sought counsel that suited his wishes but that this trait is a peculiarity that all "self-confident" people have. He wants his readers to know that Vitachuco is errant in his judgment but is gallant, self-confident, and noble in his character (161–62).

The Amerindian whose stature attracts the most attention is the *curaca* (lord) Tascaluza, who presides over a territory that Rangel calls Athahachi (290). The walled towns and chiefdoms in this territory were located in the region that became west-central Alabama. The other de Soto chroniclers also comment upon Tascaluza's physical appearance. Biedma states, "From here we headed south, drawing near the coast of New Spain (Mexico), and we passed several towns until we arrived at another province that was called Tascaluza, of which the *cacique* was an Indian so large that, to the opinion of all, he was a giant" (232). Likewise, Elvas observes that "[h]e was a man, very tall of body, large limbed, lean, and well built. He was greatly feared by his neighbors and vassals" (96). Rangel, finally, describes him as "of as tall a stature as that Antonico of the guard of the Emperor our lord, and of very good proportions, a very well built and noble man" (291). El Inca's interest in Tascaluza greatly exceeds the interest shown by the other de Soto chroniclers, Biedma, Elvas, and Rangel. In this instance, it is the native's expression that shows he is noble in spirit. El Inca states:

> La disposición de Tascaluza era, como de su hijo, que a todos sobrepujaba más de media vara en alto. Parecía gigante, o lo era, y con la altura de su cuerpo se conformaba toda la demás proporción de sus miembros y rostro. Era hermoso de cara y tenía en ella tanta severidad que en su aspecto se mostraba bien la ferocidad y grandeza de su ánimo. Tenía las espaldas conforme a su altura, y por la cintura tenía poco más de dos tercias de pretina; los brazos y piernas, derechas y bien sacadas, proporcionadas con el cuerpo. En suma, fue el indio más alto de cuerpo y más lindo de talle que estos castellanos vieron en todo lo que anduvieron de la Florida. (396)

> The build of Tascaluza was like that of his son, for he towered over all the others by more than half a *vara* [a *vara* is approximately 33 inches] and appeared to be a giant, or was one, and the rest of his body and his face were in proportion to his height. His countenance was handsome and habitually wore such a severe expression that his aspect showed well the ferocity and nobility of his spirit. His shoulders corresponded to his stature, his waist was a little more than two *tercias* around [a *tercia* is one-third of a *vara*, approximately 11 inches], his arms and legs were straight, well set and proportionate to his body. In short, he was the tallest Indian and of the finest figure that these Castilians saw in all their travels through La Florida. (328)

Civilizing discourse is apparent again as El Inca relates an observation not presented by his contemporaries. He notes that a servant of Tascaluza stands near him with a standard, or banner, that is very similar to ones carried by military units in Spain. The Spanish soldiers are, according to El Inca, very impressed to see a native military insignia for the first time on their journey (328). El Inca wants the reader to know that this great *curaca,* extraordinary in stature and noble in spirit, practices military arts comparable to those of his European counterparts. His assertion that the Spanish soldiers take note of this is offered as further proof that La Florida natives have achieved a level of civilization comparable to that of Europe.

El Inca comments expansively upon the agility and stamina exhibited by the natives; his Spanish counterparts comment narrowly upon this subject. The hyperbole rhetoric he observed in the classics is used once again to portray the La Florida natives as extraordinarily strong, courageous, and noble. In Part I of the Second Book, he devotes all of Chapter XXV to a description of how a group of Amerindians who the Spanish had pursued after a skirmish treaded water in a lake approximately thirty hours before surrendering (169–72). The thirty-hour figure probably is an exaggeration. Elvas mentions this same episode and notes that they remained overnight in the lake. To the literary scholar the issue is not the veracity of El Inca's claim, but the impression he is trying to create; in that, he succeeds brilliantly. It can be said that, although full of hyperbole and inaccuracies, El Inca's version is the most authentic for its accurate portrayal of the spirit of the Native Americans. El Inca's description of this episode, while exaggerated, is historically accurate insofar as the natives of southeastern North America were adept at swimming. All the chroniclers note that the Amerindians frequently attacked the Spanish from the safety of lakes and rivers, using the water as their "armor," knowing that the armor protecting the Spanish would sink them in this battlefield.

WAR AND WEAPONRY

Amerindian war tactics and weaponry use also receive civilizing discourse in *La Florida*. El Inca compares them with those used by the Spaniards and acknowledges that the weapons manufactured by the natives are more primitive than those of the Spanish, particularly because they lack the ability to manufacture steel, but he gives the reader the impression that the natives' weapons are, in some ways, superior to those of de Soto's soldiers because of their simplicity.

El Inca praises the military skills of the natives on an equal basis with the martial skills of de Soto and his soldiers. He tells the reader that the people of the province of Apalache, to cite one example, had a reputation among the natives of that region for martial excellence (196–97). He cites tactics that he considers to be particularly worthy of admiration, such as the hit-and-run tactics now referred to as *guerrilla* warfare, which the warriors of Apalache used to keep de Soto's technologically superior force at bay (242).

Native American archery ability impresses all the chroniclers. They all appear to be astonished by the accuracy and virtuosity of the Indians with their bows and arrows, but the European chroniclers are unable to explain how the Indians acquire these skills. El Inca, however, is able to use his mestizo experiences to give a discourse that provides the reader an explanation by stating that Native American boys begin learning how to use a bow and arrow at the age of three years (234–36).

Other chroniclers note the penetrating power of the projectiles fired by the powerful Indian bows. Cabeza de Vaca states that the Indian arrows have the power to penetrate trees. Elvas notes:

> If the arrow does not find armor, it penetrates as deeply as a crossbow. The bows are very long and the arrows are made of certain reeds like canes, very heavy and so rough that a sharpened cane passes through a shield. Some are pointed with a fish bone, as sharp as an awl, and others with a certain stone like a diamond point (59).

El Inca accurately states that the Spanish had to devise quilted armor because the arrows could penetrate their mail coats. The Amerindians soon observed that the Spaniards' plate armor "had holes in it" and that they could aim their arrows at these bare spots. An arrow shot at such a vulnerable spot by a warrior at Mauvilla gave de Soto a serious wound in the hip (341). El Inca notes that the Spanish had to devise a thick, quilted jacket to protect themselves from the skill of the native archers (236). Wise and McBride support this assertion:

> [I]t was not long before the *conquistadores* began to adopt the local armor, a jacket of cotton or maguey fibres, stuffed with cotton to a thickness of three fingers. This armor is sometimes referred to as quilted, and there must have been some stitching to keep the stuffing evenly distributed. The jackets were soaked in brine to toughen them, and were quite capable of stopping an Indian arrow or sword slash: One Spanish captain is said to have emerged from a battle looking like a porcupine, with 200 arrows in his quilted armor, and it was certainly normal for such armor to stop perhaps 10 arrows without injury to the wearer. (14)

El Inca, as with his exaggeration of the strength and stamina of the La Florida natives, offers the most detailed account of the manufacture and use of bows and arrows and describes feats of Indian archers that border on the fantastic. Cabeza de Vaca was the first chronicler to describe the Native American bows and arrows. His description lends some support to the fantastic feats claimed by El Inca, but he offers less detail. As a European, at the beginning of his narrative, he is more interested in recounting his deeds and those of his Spanish compatriots, and the New World natives are important only because of their interactions with and effects upon the Narváez expedition; thus, his description of the natives' bows is briefer than his description of their effects upon their Spanish targets.

In El Inca's description, he is preoccupied with educating the European reader about Native American culture. In Chapter IV of the First Book, El Inca offers a description in which he, once again, draws a parallel between American Indians and the "heathen" (70) of classical antiquity. He makes this comparison often because he is aware of the positive connotations such a comparison will create in the minds of those who are well read in the Western canon, as most of his readers are. He says that the Amerindians prefer bows and arrows to other weapons they have at their disposal, not only because of their effectiveness, but also "porque, para los que las traen, son de mayor gala y ornamento" (256) ("because, for those who carry them, they are the greatest embellishment and ornament"; 70). He points out that this is the reason that the ancient Greeks often depicted their deities with bows and arrows and notes that, like their European counterparts, the Native Americans engage in the supremely civilized pastime of "recreándose en sus cacerías" (256) ("the recreation of the hunt"; 70). The most interesting part of his description concerns the manufacture of the bows and the device the La Florida natives use to protect their forearms when firing, an aspect that all of his fellow chroniclers neglect to mention:

> Las cuerdas de los arcos hacen de correa de venado. Sacan del pellejo, desde la punta de la cola hasta la cabeza, una correa de dos dedos de ancho, y, después de pelada, la mojan y tuercen fuertemente, y el un cabo de ella atan a un rama de un árbol y del otro cuelgan un peso de 4 o 5 arrobas y lo dejan así hasta que se pone como una cuerda de las gruesas de vihuelón de arco, y son fortísimas. Para tirar con seguridad de que la cuerda al soltar no lastime el brazo izquierdo, lo traen guarnecido por la parte de adentro con un medio brazal, que les cubre de la muñeca hasta la sangradura, hecho de plumas gruesas y atado al brazo con una correa de venado que le da siete o ocho vueltas donde sacude la cuerda con grandísima pujanza. (256–57)

> They make the cords of the bows from deerskin, taking a strip two finger-breadths in width from the hide, running from the tip of the tail to the head. After removing the hair they dampen and twist it tightly; one end they tie to the branch of a tree, and from the other they hang a weight of four or five *arrobas* (about 25 pounds), and they leave it thus until it becomes about the thickness of the larger strings of a bass viol. These cords are extremely strong. In order to shoot safely in such a manner that when the cord springs back it may not injure the left arm, they wear as a protection on the inner side a half-bracer, which covers them from the wrist to the part of the arm that is usually bled. It is made of thick feathers and attached to the arm with a deerskin cord, which they give seven or eight turns at the place where the cord springs back most strongly. (70–71)

El Inca apparently is aware, also, of the lack of suitability of modern European firearms to the American climate and terrain because of his experiences in Peru. He recalls the Peruvian conquest and probably is aware that Alvarado had no *harquebusiers* (*harquebus* shooters) when he attacked Quito and that only one-fifth of his men were crossbowmen (Wise and McBride 9). El Inca's experiences in the Italian campaigns and the campaign to put down the Morisco rebellion, combined with his knowledge of the New World, probably give him all the background knowledge he needs to accurately appraise the performance of European weapons in the New World.

Both El Inca and Elvas note that the Spanish crossbow and the crude firearm known as the *harquebus* are outclassed by the more primitive bow of the Amerindians because of the speed with which the natives fire their arrows. They note also that the Amerindians' lack of armor protection is to their advantage because it allows them more agility than their Spanish counterparts are allowed with their heavy metal armor. As with his other descriptions of the Native Americans and their deeds, El Inca attributes greater prowess to the Native Americans than is attributed to them by his fellow chroniclers. While Elvas states, "Before a crossbowman can fire a shot, an Indian can shoot three or four arrows" (59), El Inca states that the crossbowmen and the *harquebusiers* are completely ineffective against their Indian adversaries (193). While it is unlikely that "las flechas . . . eran tantas que parecía lluvia que caía del cielo" (323) ("the arrows were so numerous that they looked like a rain falling from the skies"; 192), El Inca's description of the number of times a La Florida warrior could fire while a Spaniard was attempting to load and fire his weapon is probably accurate. The crossbow, and particularly the *harquebus,* took a notoriously long time to load. Charles Hudson, in his book *The Juan Pardo Expeditions,* states:

> Although the crossbow could fire a small missile at high velocity and could be aimed and fired by a person of little skill or strength, an experienced Indian archer could fire an arrow with comparable penetrating power (because of the heavier weight of the arrow), and he could fire several arrows in the time it took a crossbowman to load and fire a single bolt. (147)

With regard to the much more ungainly *harquebus,* Hudson states that it was

> the earliest and mechanically the crudest of the hand-held firearms. It was fired by touching a piece of lighted matchcord, like a slow-burning fuse, to the powder hole . . . A ball or shot fired from a *harquebus* had much greater velocity than an arrow or a crossbow bolt, but it was slow

to load, not very accurate, and problematic in rainy weather. Because the matchcord had to be kept alight when action might occur, great quantities of it were required. (147–48)

Wise and McBride note that the *guerrilla* warfare employed by the Native Americans, particularly in Peru, made these weapons ineffective. They note that accounts of the conquests of Peru and Mexico state that these weapons "were no longer serviceable after several weeks in the field (due to rust or broken bow strings, caused by the climate)" (8).

After several weeks of trying to use the *harquebus* in the dense and damp forests of southeastern North America, de Soto, irritated by their performance, ordered that they be destroyed and that the metal parts be melted and shaped into other equipment.

Apparently the New World terrain was unsuited to another weapon, and its site incompatibility also irritated de Soto. El Inca states:

No hemos hecho mención hasta ahora de una pieza de artillería que el gorbernador llevaba en su ejército . . . es así que, habiendo visto el adelantado que no servía sino de carga y pesadumbre, ocupando hombres que cuidasen de ella y acémilas que la llevasen, acordó dejársela al curaca Cofa para que se la guardase . . . y puédese creer que hoy la tengan en gran veneración y estima. (363)

We have not mentioned hitherto a piece of artillery the governor brought along with his army . . . the *Adelantado,* having seen that it served for nothing, except a burden and annoyance, requiring men to care for it and pack mules to transport it, decided to leave it with the *curaca* Cofa to keep for him . . . and it may be believed that they have it still, regarding it with great veneration and esteem. (264–65)

El Inca is correct to point out that the projectile arms of the La Florida natives, although more primitive than those of the Spanish, were better suited to New World warfare. Wise and McBride point out also that:

Despite their success with the arquebus in the Italian Wars, relatively few firearms were employed by the Spaniards in the New World. The long and rather unwieldy arquebus of the first half of the 16th century was a practical weapon in orderly European battles in open terrain; but it was not a weapon which could be used advantageously in the climate and terrain of the Americas. A rest was required to support the end of the barrel, a fine powder was needed for priming, and a lighted match had to be carried for ignition. The match itself was lit by flint and tinder and, since it could not be kept burning at all times, the arquebusiers in America were sometimes attacked before they could get their matches lit. (8)

The horse, the war dog, and the sword were the weapons that enabled the Spanish to outclass the Amerindians in battle. Occasionally, the Amerindians gained temporary superiority by using the woods as their "armor" as they had used the water. The Spanish could not use their horses or firepower in the thick forests, but when they could close in on the enemy and use their swords, the natives stood little chance of surviving. Wise and McBride note that:

> The second decisive factor in hand-to-hand combat with the Indians was the Spanish infantryman and his sword. At this date the . . . arquebus had not yet totally replaced the sword-and-buckler men who had built the fine reputation of the Spanish army, and who were famed throughout Europe for their skill as swordsmen. Encased in three-quarter armor and open helmet with gorget, armed with a long, double-edged sword and small buckler, these swordsmen had broken the famous Swiss pike formations which had ruled the battlefield for a century, to emerge as the leading infantrymen of the day. (14–15)

Faced with such a formidable foe, an Amerindian dressed only in a loincloth and wielding a wooden weapon that El Inca, in his typical hyperbole, refers to as a "broadsword" (70) stood no chance of survival. Wise and McBride describe the power of the Spanish sword:

> The straight Spanish sword was about a metre in length, double-edged, with a sharp point and S-shaped crossguard, one arm of which curved towards the pear-shaped pommel to protect the hand, while the other curved toward the point and could be used to trap the enemy's weapon. . . . The Spanish had gained much from the Moors when it came to sword blade manufacture, and by this date Toledo was one of the most famous centers of sword manufacture. Strict standards were enforced, and all blades were rigorously tested by bending them into an S and semicircle, and by striking full force against a steel helmet, before being passed. Toledo blades were long, strong, flexible, light, and razor-sharp—deadly weapons in the hands of skilled men, and the Spanish were the finest swordsmen in Europe. (15)

Although the hit-and-run tactics used by the natives were effective at slowing the Spanish advance, they could not stop it. Whenever the Spanish were able to take on the natives in a pitched battle, as in the battle of Mauvilla, where Tascaluza was killed and where de Soto was seriously wounded, they always prevailed. If they could not force the natives of La Florida into open combat, they simply moved on. Still, the hit-and-run tactics of the natives took their toll on de Soto and his men and were a factor in the failure of the expedition.

CLASSICAL UNIVERSALISM

The way in which El Inca presents his native characters in *La Florida* clearly exhibits his reliance upon Inca traditions in general and his awareness of the status of his mother's family as members of Inca aristocracy. He presents the reader with a who's who of the chiefs of La Florida and creates through his masterful use of narrative prose a vivid image of their deeds and personalities. In *La Florida,* he relates the deeds of both the noble and ignoble of the political and military leaders of the indigenous people.

The classical antiquities concept that humanity includes all people in all ages throughout history has a strong appeal to El Inca. He is one of the first modern writers to express the idea of the universal being. He applies this concept when he presents his Native American characters in *La Florida*. With regard to El Inca's universalist concept, Avalle-Arce has observed that this is a recurring theme in *La Florida* (20).

Amerindian leaders are portrayed in *La Florida* not as mindless savages but as astute leaders, with both noble and less-than-noble characteristics, similar to those of their European counterparts. El Inca continues to develop his theme of the Native American as a universal being, and we see his cosmic vision as he applies it to the La Florida natives. He shows parallels between Amerindian and European societies in the Third Book of *La Florida.* The noble deeds attributed to the *curaca* (chief) of Cofaqui, a La Florida province located in modern-day north-central Georgia, just as easily could have been exploits belonging to one of El Inca's Spanish ancestors. El Inca notes, with his usual hyperbole, that the chief of Cofaqui was of such noble character that he provided de Soto with four thousand natives to serve as porters and four thousand warriors to protect and guide the Spanish on their way to the neighboring province of Cofitachequi. El Inca describes the Indian military detachment and their leader, Patofa, in his customary European terms, but he also draws a parallel between this Native American society and that of his paternal homeland, building upon his universalist theme and drawing upon the mestizo experience, by noting that the Amerindian leader Patofa occupied a position similar to that of the Inca *apu,* or military officer. He then builds upon his universalist theme by noting that Patofa makes a salute to his chief that "que se diferencaba poco de la nuestra" (366) ("differs little from ours"; 269). El Inca then makes a favorable comparison between the military organization of the warriors of Cofaqui and that of de Soto's soldiers (272).

El Inca's universalist discourse is clearly evident here, but we can see also that he is aware of the limitations imposed upon him by European society. Although the Amerindian warriors are proficient, the Spanish are slightly better. El Inca realizes that he must compromise somewhat in order to avoid an official rebuke for challenging the status quo. If his *La Florida* were to be added to the Inquisition's official list of *libros prohibidos,* he would have no possibility of influencing European discourse about the Native Americans. He clearly opts for an incremental, rather than revolutionary, approach.

Another example of El Inca's universalist discourse occurs in Chapter XXV of the Third Book. He is describing the town of Mauvilla, the site of the de Soto expedition's violent encounter with the forces of the giant chief Tascaluza. If one reads carefully El Inca's description of the town's fortifications, one can see that he is describing something very similar to a walled town of medieval Europe. El Inca is trying to show that Native Americans are just as capable of building defensive fortifications as the Europeans (331). In Chapter VII of the Fourth Book, he notes that one town, Capaha, has a European-style moat around it (395).

AMERINDIAN WOMEN REMEMBERED

El Inca's idealization is not limited to his Amerindian brothers. Amerindian women are not ignored in his ennobling characterizations. He presents the female inhabitants as symbols of love and compassion just as chivalric romances present European women. He illustrates their knowledge and skills and talks about their compassion. The other de Soto chroniclers resort to their usual cursory style when they write about their encounters with New World native women. The possibility that Amerindian women could possess the qualities attributed to them by El Inca was not present in sixteenth-century European thinking.

When El Inca describes the arrival of de Soto and his army in Cofachiqui, in modern-day South Carolina, he states that this province is, uncharacteristically, ruled by a woman. He describes her in European terms as *La Señora de Cofachiqui* and draws a parallel between this episode and a similar episode from classical antiquity. El Inca's use of a classical-literature paradigm is evident when he says:

> Con este concierto pasaron el río y llegaron donde el gobernador estaba. Auto es éste bien al propio semejante, aunque inferior en grandeza y majestad, al de Cleopatra cuando por el río Cindo, en Cilicia, salió a recibir

a Marco Antonio, donde se trocaron suertes de tal manera que la que había sido acusada . . . salió por juez del que la había de condenar . . . como larga y galanamente lo cuenta todo el maestro del gran español Trajano, digno discípulo de tal maestro. (374-75)

They crossed the river in this order and came to the place where the governor was. This is an action very similar though inferior in grandeur and majesty, to that of Cleopatra when she went by the River Cydnus in Cilicia to receive Marc Anthony, where destinies were changed in such manner that she who had been accused of the crime . . . came out as judge to him who had condemned her . . . all of which is told at length by the master of that great Spaniard, Trajano, who was a worthy pupil of such a teacher. (285-86)

The other chroniclers do not describe the situation in these terms. Although they are equally impressed by the majestic beauty and serene presence of *La Señora,* their descriptions are brief and employ no European metaphors. Only El Inca describes her as a "mujer discreta y de pecho señoril" (374) ("discreet woman of noble instincts"; 285).

The most notable example concerning women occurs in the First Part of the Second Book, Chapters II and III, where El Inca narrates the relationship between the Spanish captive from the Narváez expedition, Juan Ortiz, and the daughter of Hirrihigua, his captor and tormentor. The reader is left to infer that there is a romantic relationship. El Inca highlights, also, the knowledge and skills of the native women in this section, when he notes Hirrihigua's wife and daughters help Ortiz to recover from burns, inflicted when Hirrihigua tried to roast him alive, by treating him with herbs (104). El Inca wants us to know that Ortiz is saved not only by female know-how but also by female compassion. He emphasizes that Ortiz is saved and ultimately escapes only through the intervention of the chief's wife and three daughters.

EL INCA'S LITERARY ORIENTATION

Since one of El Inca's stated objectives in writing *La Florida* is to honor the heroism and bravery of both the Spanish explorers and the Indians, and since the chivalric novels and epic poems of the Middle Ages had such an influence upon him in his formative years, it is only logical that he should refer to his Amerindian characters as "*cavalleros.*" It is clear that El Inca wishes the Amerindians to be thought as worthy of esteem and praise as the virtuous heroes of the *novelas de caballería* (novels about knights). This was a comparison he knew his audience could grasp, since we know from such contemporary works as *Don Quijote* that such novels were in vogue in middle to late sixteenth-century Spain. Given these factors, it is logical that El Inca would utilize the expository methods of the medieval chroniclers to relate his interpretation of the de Soto expedition.

Quesada asserts that El Inca's treatment of the Amerindian characters is one of the key aspects that reveals to us his literary intent and orientation (352). Quesada, too, supports the idea that chivalric romances influenced El Inca's writing style, despite El Inca's protestations to the contrary. He notes in particular the episode of the ordeal of Juan Ortiz. While other chroniclers describe the episode "*ligeramente*" ("in a cursory manner"), El Inca narrates the scene like a novelist, with details reminiscent of novels of chivalry. He notes that El Inca's description of the Temple of Tolomeco, located in Cofachiqui, is evocative of the descriptive style used by medieval authors to describe "los palacios en las novelas de caballería" (352) ("palaces in novels of chivalry"). He points out that Rangel mentions only the riches found there, and Elvas doesn't mention it at all. The assertion that El Inca is attempting to alter the predominant discourse on Amerindians is evident to Quesada.

Modern scholars have criticized El Inca for attributing classical-style discourse to the natives of North America. This is a valid criticism from the perspective of the historian, but viewing El Inca's work from the perspective of a literary scholar, Quesada notes that embellishment is part of El Inca's style (153) and, as noted previously, it is consistent with his objective of initiating an alternative discourse on the cultural hybridization of the New World experience. He agrees that *La Florida* is not just a recitation of events but represents both "la crítica y la creación" (153) ("criticism and creation")—"crítica" because El Inca is criticizing, although implicitly, the way the Spanish relate to the natives of the New World, and "creación" because El Inca is creating a new discourse that is adequate for the task of communicating the process of creation caused by the intersection of the Old World and the New World. Through his paradigm of universal man, he is trying to establish a place in society for the marginalized mestizo. *La Florida,* then, should be viewed as a history with a purpose, and as such we should read it primarily for what it tells us about El Inca, his class, his place in society, and society's perception of him as a representative of an alien race. Quesada observes that El Inca does not fictionalize so much as he amplifies the story to make an intellectual point (352).

Although historians such as George Bancroft have criticized the historical accuracy of El Inca's work because he interjects novelistic devices that, at times, give the work a fantasy tone, without these novelistic approaches, the lasting impression of the Amerindians that El Inca wants to present to the reader is not possible. The way in which El Inca narrates scenes that illustrate Native

American courage and valor has received repeated criticism from historians. The influence of the Spanish medieval epic style is evident. One can see evidence of this in the noble behavior of some of the Amerindian characters who seem to observe a code of honor that greatly resembles the chivalric code of the Middle Ages.

Some scenes, according to the critics, appear to have been taken straight from the chivalric romances. The unexpected events that befall the de Soto expedition, such as violent storms and shipwrecks, and nearly disastrous judgmental errors that conclude with a positive resolution of events, all contribute to the chivalric tone. In Chapter XIX of the Sixth Book, El Inca describes the arrival of the de Soto expedition in Mexico. In true epic fashion, de Soto's men recount their adventures in La Florida, and El Inca notes that the viceroy and his court "espantáronse de la disposición de gigante que el cacique Tascaluza tenía" (517) ("were astonished to hear of the gigantic size of the cacique Tascaluza"; 547).

While the epic tone in *La Florida* might be problematic for the student of history because of a need to confirm the facts, for the student of literature, the important characteristic is that El Inca creates the impression that the native peoples who confront de Soto on his voyage of exploitation are of a profoundly courageous and valorous character, a fact that even the fastidious historian cannot deny.

One can criticize El Inca from a historical perspective for idealizing a particular group, but one should remember that he is trying to provide a counterargument to a popular conception that is one-hundred-percent negative. One should consider, as well, that El Inca does not shrink from honestly presenting certain character flaws on the part of the Amerindians that get them into trouble from time to time. For this reason, one can argue that El Inca's tendencies toward idealization are misinterpreted and overemphasized by his critics. Quesada presents a more accurate view when he notes that this tendency is caused, in part, by the spiritual kinship El Inca feels toward the natives of the New World (352).

El Inca's psychological portraits of his characters and perceptive ruminations on the human condition fit nicely into the tradition of the old Spanish chroniclers. Like the chroniclers of old, El Inca delights in the art of his narrative as much as its history. His descriptions of the natives, their towns and dwellings, and their manner of living are vivid and detailed, even though some details are the product of the author's active imagination.

In his writing about the Amerindians, El Inca shows his loyalty to his ancestral heritage by alternating between the heroism of the Spanish *caballeros* and the courage shown by the Native Americans. This alternation and the epic style in which the events are described have led the venerable Peruvian critic Ventura García Calderón to declare that *La Florida* is "una *Araucana* en prosa" (30) ("an *Araucana* in prose").

El Inca insists that *La Florida* is historically accurate from cover to cover. To underscore this assertion, he emphasizes his use of the Carmona and Coles narratives. His self-proclaimed critical inquiry includes rejecting certain passages from the two narratives because the authors did not indicate in which provinces certain events occurred (248). It is obvious that El Inca is determined that the reader accept his narrative as fact, including his sympathetic portrayal of Native Americans.

El Inca tells us, from the beginning, that this is *La Florida del Inca*. Another reason for his including "del Inca" ("of the Inca") in his title is to inform the reader, from the beginning, that his account can be relied upon because the author, half Native American, half Spanish, is uniquely qualified to interpret these events. As a mestizo, he has experiences of Native American life upon which he can draw to create an impression of believability. His repeated affirmations of his Native American lineage within the prologue and the narrative itself support this hypothesis. The subtitle to *La Florida del Inca* provides further insight into El Inca's approach to authorship: *Historia del Adelantado Hernando de Soto, Governador y Capitán General del Reyno de La Florida y de otros heroicos cavalleros Españoles e Yndios* (*History of the Adelantado Hernando de Soto, Governor and Captain-General of the Kingdom of La Florida and of Other Heroic Gentlemen, Spaniards and Indians*).

El Inca's authority as interpreter and conveyor of reality comes also from the means by which he relates his narrative. At a time when so many Europeans could neither read nor write, and the printed book was still a new invention, the written word ensures authority and credibility that no longer exists, now that writing and printing are commonplace. The people of the sixteenth century believed that when something appeared in print it was very likely true. One need look only to the *Quijote* text to see how Cervantes lampooned this tendency through his created character, Don Quijote, the would-be knight errant.

In the context of our times, the attempt to influence public opinion through embellishment of the facts is called propaganda; however, one must remember the sixteenth-century context in which El Inca wrote. In those days, there was no distinction between history and propaganda—the historical writers of that era usually were motivated by more than a desire to create an objective description of historical fact. They wanted to sell a viewpoint. El Inca's fellow chronicler, Cabeza de Vaca, is an excellent example. The publication of his *Naufragios* was part of a lobbying campaign by the author to win a pension for his service in the New World. El Inca's motivations included a sincere desire to save a group of his fellow Native Americans from their pagan beliefs, ennoble their reputation, and ensure that their courage and heroic acts were included in history. When one considers El Inca within the context of his times, one can conclude that his goals are laudable and thus forgive the slightly deceptive tools he uses to accomplish them.

Positive historical acknowledgment and cultural preservation are not El Inca's only goals concerning the Amerindians. He is sensitive to the Spanish insensitivity toward the Native American, having experienced this callousness in his own life. He wants the Spaniards to change their attitudes and to stop excluding and exploiting them. He hopes to persuade the Spanish government to colonize La Florida and to educate the natives, both spiritually and intellectually.

Some historians believe that El Inca's revolutionary challenge to Spain's status quo probably contributed to the reason *La Florida*'s publisher, Pedro Crasbeeck, declined to publish a second edition, in spite of the commercial success of the first edition. His pleas that respect and equitable treatment be extended to the colonies, to the natives, and to their culture go unheeded, and the situation ultimately resolves itself in the Latin American revolutionary upheavals of the early nineteenth century.

With his classical rhetoric and epic ruminations, El Inca succeeds in his mission to rehabilitate the popular European image of the Amerindian. He conveys reality, even though many details are not correct. Zamora underscores this view when she points out that El Inca's representation of the native peoples of La Florida results in "the transformation of the figure of the native as an ignorant savage, common in earlier accounts, into that of a wise leader, eloquent orator, and gallant warrior, an equal to the best Europe had to offer" (42). Leonard supports this assertion also when he observes:

> By the varied literary devices he employed, El Inca was not consciously falsifying his account but was merely accepting current techniques of Renaissance craftsmanship which followed models of antiquity. Despite its excess artistic baggage, *The Florida of the Inca* remains essentially what it purports to be—a graphic, documented recital of an astounding feat of human courage and endurance. By poetic distortion the Inca gives a deeper understanding of the reality of the . . . de Soto expedition and of its tragic futility than does the more unvarnished testimony of actual participants—a fact that helped to win this work an accolade as "the first great classic of American history." ("The Inca," 58)

Although El Inca's descriptions are at times idealized, they reveal the cosmic, universal theme that both Spaniards and Amerindians are human beings who merit the same consideration and respect and who display the same intelligence as all the peoples of the world. Since the allegorical *caballero novelesco* (novelistic knight) epitomizes culture, courtesy, and courage, the hallmarks of the European idea of civilization, El Inca attributes to the American natives these virtues by comparing their actions with those of their Spanish contemporaries and to those of the old heroes. He praises the Amerindian's noble character and cites outstanding behavior. He is pointing out that, in spite of obvious cultural differences, we are all more similar than we might imagine. He wants the reader to know that human dignity is something that transcends national boundaries.

La Florida is important because of its poetic and epic tone (unique for a work of prose) and because it captures both the spirit of Native America and the spirit of European America; in sum, in *La Florida,* El Inca captures the very essence of the American colonial experience. His approach to the European side of that experience is the subject of the next chapter.

4
La Florida's *Ideal Conquerors*

The way in which El Inca depicts the Spaniards and their misadventures in North America provides the reader with a view into the mestizo author's European perspective. As he states in his prologue, one purpose in writing *La Florida* is to record the *hazañas* (heroic acts) of de Soto and his soldier-explorers and to recount the hardships they suffered for the honor and fame of the Spanish nation. El Inca's purpose is not only to extol the virtues of Spain and its conquering heroes. He is attempting to create a model of behavior to which his countrymen can aspire, thereby creating a new, more humane colonization experience.

El Inca's approach to his treatment of his Spanish characters is not subtle. He comments continuously on the vices and virtues (primarily virtues) of the soldiers of what is at the time the most powerful military in western Europe as they set out to win fame and fortune (primarily fortune) and subjugate new peoples and territories for God and *patria* (homeland). El Inca extols the courage of de Soto's men as freely and with as much pride as he extols the positive characteristics of the Native Americans. El Inca's *mestizaje* (mestizo status) is evident when he proclaims, commenting upon the battle of Mauvilla, in which de Soto's forces defeated the forces of the duplicitous Tascaluza, that they called upon God to give them courage in this desperate situation, following the example of their conquering ancestors (348). It is the "ánimo invincible" (407) ("invincible spirit"; 348) that El Inca seeks to emphasize in *La Florida,* ennobling the images of the Spanish soldiers and, indirectly, ennobling himself in public perception.

El Inca is as acutely aware of his aristocratic Spanish heritage as he is of his aristocratic Amerindian heritage. Not only is he the hidalgo Captain Sebastian Garcilaso's son, but he is the celebrated Andalucian fighter Captain Alonso de Vargas's nephew also. These relationships create within El Inca a keen awareness of his "noble" status within Spanish society. He knows that he has kin, however distant, who have excelled in both arms and letters. His soldier-poet namesake and distant cousin is the most outstanding example.

Although he states repeatedly in *La Florida* that his status as an "Indian" makes him supremely qualified to comment upon Native American society, he is confident that his familiarity with things Spanish makes him equally qualified to comment upon the exploits of de Soto and his soldiers. Without diminishing the importance of his royal Native American ancestry, he brings to his writing a great sense of Spanish *patria* (patriotism); he emphasizes for the reader the glory of the Spanish Empire, however subjective this glory may be. Although a sense of Native American resentment toward the superimposed hispanicism of the New World is at times perceptible, El Inca's medieval Spanish and classical influences lead him to exalt the heroic acts of the Spanish explorers. This is a characteristic that will be seen again in El Inca's *Historia general del Perú*.

The pre-Renaissance chivalric romances that entertained the young Garcilaso and suggested thoughts and attitudes that became prevalent in society in sixteenth-century Spain prompted El Inca to emphasize Spanish actions and abilities with arms with the same vehemence with which he encouraged Spanish settlements and European agriculture in Florida. The chivalric romantic medieval mentality afflicted Spanish society much longer than other European countries, and its eventual application to Spanish colonial life contributed to the gross mismanagement of the Spanish colonies. In comparison, other European countries that excluded the medieval mentality in their approach to their colonies escaped the consequential outcomes that Spain experienced. The *encomienda* system was nothing more than a New World version of the feudal system of medieval Europe (Leonard, *Brave*, 6). The Spanish aristocrats' disdain for honest work ensured the social and economic decline of the colonies that followed the conquest:

> In the form of *encomiendas*, he (the *conquistador*) derived the benefits of the toil of the conquered as a legitimate reward for bringing them into the Christian fold; his position as a feudal lord was a mark of divine gratitude for his military prowess while the manual labor of his serfs was proper punishment for their allegiance to a false faith. Toward the Jews, forced into the role of money changers and middlemen by the circumstances of their existence, the Spanish felt a similar disdain . . . he viewed with contempt the profitable careers which the growing capitalism of the modern age offered him through the development of these pursuits. Hence, with industry, agriculture, and finance bearing the marks of the loss of Christianity, and with God apparently favoring the forward sweep

of Spanish arms, the one true path to glory and material rewards was that of soldier. (Leonard, *Brave*, 6)

This, above all, is the perspective reflected in the Hispanic side of El Inca's writing.

DE SOTO: EL INCA'S *MODELO IDEAL*

As the leader of the La Florida expedition, Hernando de Soto is the figure upon whom El Inca centers the European perspective of his narrative. To El Inca, de Soto is the *modelo ideal* (ideal model) of the Spanish explorer. Biedma, Elvas, and Rangel, in their chronicles, present de Soto in positive terms, but El Inca is the only de Soto chronicler who describes his exploits with such enthusiasm and detail. El Inca wants to show his patriotism and appeal to his Spanish audience by portraying the Captain General of *La Florida* as a nobleman, but his pride in his kinship to de Soto, as well as his desire to give his fellow Spaniards a portrayal of humane behavior, probably contributed equally to this portrayal.

De Soto is the epitome of bravery and courage throughout *La Florida*. The episode in Chapter XXIV of Book II, Part I, is such an illustration. Ambushed by the treacherous Floridian cacique Vitachuco, de Soto takes charge of the situation, mounting a frontal assault on horseback against his Indian adversaries, in the manner of the *caballeros* (knights) of old, because de Soto was always the first one into the fight (167). While idealizing de Soto through liberal use of hyperbole, El Inca's representation of this particular aspect of de Soto's character is probably accurate (Lockhart 190–92). El Inca records this encounter using words that show de Soto as supremely courageous, in the tradition of El Cid, as well as supremely astute. Suspecting a trap, de Soto, before going forth to meet Vitachuco, strategically pre-positions men and horses and, upon the signal of one of his men firing a *harquebus*, launches a preemptive strike that saves the day (167). In other passages, El Inca uses equally positive descriptions. In the Second Book, Part II, Chapter X, El Inca praises de Soto for fighting (El Cid–style) with great courage and encouraging his men by calling out to them by name (212).

Along with courage and astuteness, El Inca emphasizes de Soto's military discipline. In Book III, Chapter XXXVI, de Soto and his men are in their 1540 winter camp. The Chicaha Indians (probably located in what is now northern Mississippi), attack the camp. El Inca reports that de Soto was the first to respond because he always slept in his armor in order to be prepared for an attack (367). El Inca concludes this chapter by pointing out once again the bravery and martial discipline of de Soto, just in case his readers missed it the first time (368).

Historians have noted that El Inca's image of de Soto is overly positive. Given the disastrous outcome of the expedition, one could hardly argue with this assertion. Paul Hoffman, in his brief biography of de Soto that appears in Volume 1 of *The De Soto Chronicles*, argues for a more realistic interpretation of de Soto's behavior:

> In sum, one has to agree with Raul Porrás Barrenechea that de Soto was "neither better nor worse than other *conquistadores* nor in any way a paradigm of goodness or gentleness." Garcilaso and romantic writers who have followed his lead would have it otherwise, but a close reading of the available record shows us a man who delighted in his skill with a horse and lance when used against other human beings, was ambitious and greedy, and, in the view of contemporaries who knew him well, passionate and curt in his behavior toward others. Such a person would not be welcomed in the dens of many who, knowing only the romantic image, continue to idealize Hernando de Soto. (459)

Besides martial skill and courage, another aspect of El Inca's de Soto is chivalry, again in the tradition of the medieval Spanish epic. When considering El Inca's distorted view of de Soto, one must remember that he is trying to create an image in the mind of the reader—the image that de Soto is the ideal Spanish explorer. El Inca's de Soto represents the ideal balance between ruthlessness and reason, between martial astuteness and human compassion. He is a *modelo* based upon the behavior of the chivalric heroes of medieval Spain. While El Inca's representation of de Soto is something of a construct, there is some agreement among historians that there is at least a little truth to the idea that de Soto was more chivalric on the La Florida expedition than he had been during his youthful forays into Central and South America. Even Hoffman admits:

> And once returned to Spain (after his adventure in Peru), where his role as a leading commander in Pizarro's forces was well advertised, he apparently fitted into court life without difficulties, only to find that he was again treated like a subordinate when his petitions for a known, profitable governorship were denied. But he maintained his . . . lavish household, putting a bold face on what must have been something of a disappointment. This behavior and his generally moderate conduct in La Florida toward the Indians (compared with his actions in Central America) suggest some moderation of his personality with age. (458–59)

The important aspect, from the perspective of a literary scholar, is El Inca's description of de Soto and how that description fits into the context of El Inca's narrative. As previously noted, El Inca is attempting to create a context for more humane and equitable interactions between Amerindians and Spaniards. With this in mind, as well as the fact that de Soto is a distant relative of El Inca, one can understand the overwhelmingly positive representation of a man who is in reality not what one could call a positive role model. El Inca is trying to give the reader an object lesson in chivalric behavior, so the de Soto of *La Florida* is, one can argue, almost an allegorical figure. He is like the idealistic heroes of the medieval epics.

El Inca's descriptions of de Soto's physical stature and character suggest to the reader a passage from El Cid or some other medieval epic. Like El Cid and other virtuous medieval heroes, El Inca's de Soto is constantly preoccupied with the welfare of his men. De Soto's martial prowess is matched by the nobility of his ancestry, since El Inca states that he is "hijodalgo de todos cuatro costados" (462) ("an *hidalgo* through all four lines"; 447). His physical characteristics, as described by El Inca, are also worthy of the hero of the Spanish epic: handsome, strong, and skilled in horsemanship (447).

In order to reinforce his representation of de Soto in the mind of the reader, El Inca once again utilizes the classical humanist rhetorical device of citing eyewitnesses to back up his narrative. El Inca describes de Soto's arrival in Santiago de Cuba after King Charles V had named him governor, captain-general, and *adelantado* of Cuba and La Florida, noting that the citizens received him with much joy and celebration because of his excellent reputation (264–65). El Inca is saying that the reader should believe his representation of de Soto because the reaction of the people of Cuba to de Soto's presence proves that his is a true-to-life representation. De Soto's fame as a good man and skillful soldier had, according to El Inca, preceded him.

When El Inca describes de Soto's actions in battle, his narrative once again reads more like a medieval epic poem than a chronicle of the colonial period. The use of the epic style is one characteristic that has led scholars to refer to *La Florida* as the *Araucana* in prose. Consider again, for example, the episode of Book II, Part I, Chapter XXIV, when the native cacique Vitachuco tries to ambush de Soto and take him prisoner. De Soto, in El Cid–like manner, mounts a horse and charges headlong into a squadron of Vitachuco's men, routing the native force (167). Just in case the reader missed the point, El Inca reinforces his Cid-like representation of de Soto with the editorial comment, "no deben ser caudillos tan arriscados" (309) ("leaders ought not to be so bold"; 167). This passage and others like it leave the reader with the impression that de Soto embodies the Spanish military tradition. He is prudent, brave, wise, and an inspiring leader. To give credibility to this aspect of his narrative, El Inca once again resorts to his classical rhetorical tool of referring to an authority on the facts. El Inca quotes Alonso de Carmona as saying that de Soto was very experienced in Amerindian warfare (252). Although there is doubt as to whether the Carmona document ever existed, the important thing is that El Inca expects the reader to believe the document is real, thereby giving credibility to his version of the facts.

Even when El Inca relates an example of poor judgment on de Soto's part, he frames it in such a way that the reader is left with the impression the error was not entirely de Soto's fault. An excellent example occurs in Book III, Chapter XXXIII, when El Inca presents de Soto's fateful decision to go farther inland after the Battle of Mauvilla instead of going to the Gulf Coast to rendezvous with the resupply ships at Achusi. El Inca cannot ignore this, since it was the direct cause of the ultimate destruction of the expedition, but El Inca presents it as an overreaction to a mutiny plot by some of de Soto's men (356). El Inca presents de Soto more as a victim of the greed and materialism of his men than as an individual whose own greed and conceit cause him to commit serious errors in judgment. With regard to the disastrous decision to forego resupplying the expedition and move farther inland, El Inca presents de Soto as a victim of circumstance, though he cannot help but acknowledge the stupidity of the decision. De Soto arrives at his decision after learning of a plot among his troops to leave La Florida on the resupply ships. El Inca implies that de Soto is brought to his decision by a combination of the treachery of his men and his own *pundonor,* or Spanish sense of chivalric honor (357).

EL INCA WRITES IN THE CHIVALRIC STYLE

The idealization of de Soto is not surprising given the literary conventions of the day. Pastor notes that the image of the *conquistador* as a brave, wise, and benevolent father figure begins in the earliest part of the colonial period through works such as the *Cartas de relación* by Cortés:

> Hay que señalar que ese modelo que estaba en el centro de los procesos de ficcionalización de la realidad de la conquista que encontrábamos en textos como los *Cartas de Relación* [de Cortés] o—desde un enfoque ligeramente distinto—la *Historia Verdadera* de Bernal Díaz, estaba igualmente presente, aunque a veces de forma menos explícita, en los textos fundamentales . . . *Las Ordenanzas de Gobierno* de Hernán Cortés, por ejemplo, presentan una continuidad del mito creado en las *Cartas,* de la figura del conquistador justo, cristiano y paternal, cuya figura modélica proyecta más allá de las *Cartas* mismas. (447–48)

One must remember that this model that was at the center of the processes of fictionalization of the reality of the conquest, which we find in texts

like the *Letters of Report* [of Cortés] or—from a distinct perspective—the
True History by Bernal Díaz, was also present, although at times less ob-
viously, in the founding documents of the colonies . . . the *Laws of Government* of Hernán Cortés, for example, present a continuation of the
myth created in the *Letters,* that of the just, Christian, and paternal conqueror, whose ideal figure is projected by the *Letters.*

Pastor notes also that the representation of the *conquistador* as the ultimate
action hero is due to the influence of the medieval Spanish chroniclers who
blended fact with fiction in narratives that were based upon actual events
(99–100).

Leonard also cites evidence of the tremendous influence medieval epics exerted upon sixteenth-century Spain when he observes:

Much more direct evidence of the reading of the romances of chivalry
by the conquistadors is supplied by that prince of chroniclers, a soldier
in the conquering ranks of Cortés army—Bernal Díaz del Castillo. In his
famous *True History of the Conquest of New Spain,* which is a first-hand
account of the Spanish campaigns . . . and which, in some passages itself
reads like a novel of chivalry, the soldier-author records the profound impression that the first glimpse of the Aztec capital in the beautiful valley
in Mexico produced on the approaching Spanish troops. . . . Where the
plural "we" is employed it clearly indicates that Bernal Díaz, in alluding
to the comparison of the scene . . . with descriptions found in *Amadis of
Gaul* and its successors, did not express himself in terms of his own reading alone, but was conveying an impression shared by his companions
who were also familiar with these novels. (*Brave,* 42–43)

Evidence of this type of influence in El Inca's writing is not surprising given
his youthful interest in novels of chivalry. Leonard points out that novels of
chivalric tales of knight errantry were so popular in sixteenth-century Spain
that even prominent religious figures like Santa Teresa de Jesús enjoyed reading
them. El Inca probably was no exception:

With varying degrees of credence, then, these romantic stories were read
and accepted by the religious and lay alike, and the writers and poets of
both groups were consciously or subconsciously influenced by this popular literature in their own artistic expression. Even in far-off Cuzco, the
ancient seat of the Inca civilization in the lofty Sierra of Peru where the
Conquistador had introduced this fiction, a youthful mestizo, offspring
of a Spanish conqueror and an Incan princess, was steeping himself in

chivalric narratives; this was Garcilaso de la Vega—el Inca, as he was called—who was to write the first truly American work . . . Long afterwards he shamefacedly admitted this early fondness which, he claimed, was changed to aversion by reading the thundering denunciation of these entertaining books in the preface of Pedro Mexía's learned *Historia Imperial.* (Leonard, *Brave,* 23–24)

The chivalric novel of the sixteenth century was a new genre that encompassed and built upon the tradition of the medieval Spanish chronicle, thus creating an aura of believability in the mind of the sixteenth-century reader—or listener, as these tales frequently were read aloud to those who could not read or write. Illiteracy was a widespread problem in sixteenth-century Europe. Leonard observes:

The popularity of these romances in the sixteenth-century was, in reality, a more democratic revival in the Spanish Peninsula of a medieval passion for the literature of chivalry. The folk ballads, which belonged to the whole people and still retained the affection of the less cultivated at the time of the Conquest, contained some of the same fanciful and idealistic elements, but rivaling them in appeal among the more aristocratic classes were the newer forms of chronicles purporting to give historical accounts of the past. As the Moorish frontier . . . was pushed farther south, these prose chronicles took on more and more a picturesque flavor. In time they were dominated by a spirit of poetic invention and chivalry which blended fact and fiction indistinguishably. Hence the chivalric romances were but a step further and they reappeared with something of the aura of authenticity enveloping the contemporary chronicle. The multiplying agency of the printing press could not fail to make this revival far more widespread and influential, for the circulation of these romantic tales was no longer limited by the manuscript form to the wealthy aristocracy. (*Brave,* 14)

Dowling asserts that novels of chivalry exert the greatest influence upon El Inca's narrative: "*La Florida* invites comparison with the romances of chivalry at various levels of inscription, and in fact probably owes more to the 'rejected' chivalresque romances than to any other literary genre" (106). Dowling refers to the chivalric novels as "rejected" because their influence upon the Spanish society became so pervasive that both government and church leaders attempted to outlaw their dissemination. El Inca, himself, as noted previously, claims to have rejected his youthful enthusiasm for such books, despite the fact that their influence is present in his writings:

At the most basic level of *La Florida del Inca*—that of texture—aspects of the chivalresque model underlie much of the linguistic register in which narrator and characters address, respectively, the reader and one another, as well as the congeries of images appearing in descriptive and narrative passages. (Dowling 107)

As for El Inca's self-confessed affinity for tales of chivalry, followed by his alleged rejection of them, Dowling points out that, "with respect to Garcilaso's denunciation of the romances, . . . in Garcilaso as in Cervantes, the chivalresque spirit of adventure is first rejected and then readmitted in another guise, under a more idealized rationale" (143). Thus, El Inca's de Soto behaves more like the idealized heroes of sixteenth-century novels such as *Amadis of Gaul* than the greedy opportunist that he was. It is the influence of the chivalresque that, according to Dowling, causes El Inca to represent de Soto and his troops as "knights," as well as the Native Americans who fight the Spanish because they, too, are seeking to uphold a code of honor (108). El Inca's de Soto is, like Pastor's *modelo*, "justo, cristiano y paternal" (448) ("just, Christian, and paternal"), as one can see in the text of *La Florida*. El Inca presents de Soto as a leader whose wisdom and judgment make him a beloved figure to his troops. Consider, for example, the scene in which de Soto greets Pedro Calderón, one of his subordinate officers, and 119 of his troops after they had been separated from the main part of the expedition for a few months. According to El Inca, de Soto receives them like a father, and the soldiers act as if they are in the presence of a father figure (243). Scenes like this are characteristic of the *modelo* of the *conquistador,* as articulated by Pastor, that is present in most of the chronicles of the colonial period. By representing de Soto as an idealized type based on the heroes of medieval Spanish literature, El Inca is conforming to the literary conventions of his day.

Another aspect of the representation, one that is related to El Inca's attempt to create a more humane colonization, is de Soto's capacity for compassion, which is as great as the other virtues that El Inca insists de Soto possesses. To support this characterization, El Inca uses the episode in Book II, Part I, Chapter XXVI, involving three Amerindians who fight de Soto and his men with particular bravery. After their capture, they explain to de Soto the Native American tradition of not surrendering in battle, even to save one's own life. El Inca reports that de Soto is deeply affected by the eloquence and earnestness of their statements, so much so that he decides to set them free (174). Here, not only do we see El Inca represent de Soto as a person of great compassion, but also once again he employs the paternalistic imagery seen throughout his narrative.

El Inca writes that de Soto shows his benevolent attitude toward the natives who decline to make war against him. When the Spanish enter the chiefdom of Coosa, in modern-day northern Georgia, the cacique of the region offers de Soto and his troops the opportunity to establish a settlement in the province. El Inca tells us that de Soto is so impressed by such generosity on the part of the cacique that he expresses a sense of obligation in his reply, promising to return and make a settlement as soon as circumstances permit (325).

Another chivalric characteristic that El Inca incorporates into his representation of de Soto and his troops is the concept of fame and fortune. Like the knights errant of old, de Soto and his men set out for a strange land in search of the riches that are rumored to be there. Consider, for example, the passage from Book I, Chapter V, where El Inca notes that, in 1538, de Soto generated a tremendous response by publicizing throughout the Iberian Peninsula his scheme to explore La Florida (72–73). The theme of fame and fortune continues when de Soto and the expedition arrive in Cuba and meet a wealthy and well-connected aristocrat who, in spite of his advanced years, also expresses great interest in accompanying de Soto on his expedition to seek fame and fortune in La Florida (88). Later in Book I, El Inca notes that although the hardships that de Soto and his men encounter in La Florida are great, they are able to persevere because of their desire to maintain their honor (82).

Although the expedition is a failure and de Soto loses his life because of his own bad judgment, El Inca represents it as one of the most heroic episodes of Spanish exploration in the New World. He emphasizes that the de Soto expedition was the most well financed and well organized of any Spanish expedition launched during the sixteenth century. The failure of the expedition, according to El Inca, in no way diminishes the great feats of arms and endurance that the *adelantado* from Extremadura and his intrepid band accomplished.

CHRISTIAN VALOR IN THE SPANISH CHARACTER

For El Inca, the valorous behavior of the Christians is so self-evident that numerous editorial comments about it are not necessary. He makes only a few observations on this theme, such as in Book II, Part I, Chapter XIV, when Gonzalo Silvestre and Juan López make a difficult return to the expedition's base camp after accompanying de Soto and a small scouting party that was attempting to find a way to cross the Great Swamp near the town of Urribarracuxi. After the party succeeds in finding a crossing, Silvestre and López must return to the camp and inform Luis de Moscoso, whom de Soto had left in charge, to bring up the rest of the troops and supplies. The two young explorers face trials and dangers on their night-long journey that would befit a hero of a chivalric novel on a quest to prove his valor. Near the end of the chapter, El Inca notes their bravery in one of his few editorial comments on the subject of Spanish valor, saying that their bravery in winning the New World for their king has brought them material wealth and has brought the natives spiritual wealth in the form of Catholicism (139). When Silvestre and López are near the camp, they come under attack from the natives and are rescued by a small force of horsemen led by a particularly valiant soldier named Nuño Tovar. El Inca reflects on the valor of the Spanish nation through his representation of Tovar, rather than through direct editorial comment (139).

Catholicism is another important part of El Inca's representation of the de Soto expedition. The theme of religious purpose is another example of the chivalresque that pervades El Inca's work. His frequent allusions to divine providence are reminiscent of *Amadis of Gaul* and other chivalric novels published in the sixteenth century, which, themselves, reflect ideas from medieval epics like *El Cid:*

> These books of knighthood embrace Christian ideology reaching all the way back to the First Crusade and abounding in the epic poems of that and slightly later eras, as well as the *romanceros,* or compilations of ballads, dating from the fourteenth and fifteenth centuries. . . . After the final rout of the Moors from Granada and the expulsion of Spain's Jews at the end of the fifteenth century, the concept of true nobility tended to become equated with the "uncontaminated bloodlines" of the victorious faction and therefore with the Christian warrior and Servant of the Catholic Monarchs. Thus, echoes of the medieval chivalresque integrated themselves into Spain's emerging national consciousness. The continuing appeal of the old archetypes was easily transferred . . . to the bold and hearty conquistadors of the Indies, who perceived themselves as providentially selected to carry out the next stage of their country's "sacred mission"—this time in America. (Dowling 107)

While it is true that the sense of religious purpose that is pervasive in *La Florida* is characteristic of the influence that the chivalresque novel exerted on El Inca, the other source of this aspect of El Inca's representation of his characters is El Inca's own sincere belief in the redemptive power of Catholicism. El Inca was a member of an order of lay workers and was very active in religious work, officiating at baptisms, participating in charitable work, and serving as an administrator of a church-run hospital in his home district of Montilla.

The primary objective of the conquest, for El Inca, is the diffusion of Catholicism throughout the Americas. Not only does El Inca emphasize repeatedly throughout *La Florida* the need for the conversion of the Indians, but he repeats his own faith and dedication to the Church as well. Perhaps, as a mestizo, he feels that European Catholics might look upon him with suspicion in the same way they view the Jews of the Iberian Peninsula who elected to convert rather than accept exile. The pressure exerted upon those who were not of the "uncontaminated" class by the inquisitorial fanaticism that dominated Spain at that time caused individuals of mixed heritage to feel compelled to constantly proclaim their fidelity to Catholicism. This state of religious oppression creates an environment in which marginalized figures like El Inca feel a kinship with other persecuted minorities. One can see evidence of this in his translation of the *Dialoghi di amore.* Hebreo's work is the product of the religious philosophy of the Jewish people, and El Inca's desire to translate and interpret the work for a Spanish audience is a result of the spiritual anxiety of the mestizo condition in the sixteenth century.

From the beginning of *La Florida,* El Inca emphasizes the religious objective of the conquest. Consider, for example, the passage from the prologue in which El Inca states emphatically that the principal motivation for settling La Florida is to spread the Catholic faith. El Inca contends that, through writing *La Florida,* he, too, is making a contribution to the great religious mission he believes the Spanish nation was chosen by God to perform. The same idea of a Christian mission for what is, in reality, a vain attempt to accumulate wealth through ruthless exploitation of the Native American population, appears again and again throughout the narrative. One reads passages that give an idea of a divine purpose for the expedition so often that they become almost formulaic in their frequency. In Book I, Chapter I, for example, El Inca states that he is writing *La Florida* "para la Gloria y honra de la Santísima Trinidad, Dios Nuestro Señor, y con deseo del aumento de su Santa Fe Católica y de la corona de España" (251) ("for the glory and honor of the Most Holy Trinity, God, our Lord, and with the desire of advancing His holy Catholic faith and the Crown of Spain"; 61). El Inca, through the repetition of allusions to religious purpose, is attempting to promote a continuation of the evangelizing mission that he contends was the most important function of the de Soto expedition. When one considers the startling contrast between El Inca's evangelizing vision and the brutal reality of events as they occurred, one must remember that he is thinking in terms of the ideal. He is attempting to create a paradigm for others to emulate in order to create conditions for the ultimate settlement of La Florida that will avoid the cruelty and exploitation that were so prevalent in his native Peru. He asserts repeatedly that he writes to motivate his native countrymen to colonize North America with the objective of preaching the Gospel to the native population (521).

El Inca tells the reader that, although chosen by divine providence to carry out an evangelizing mission, de Soto does not achieve the spiritual conquest that El Inca sees as the primary objective of colonization. As El Inca relates the episode in Book III, Chapter XIX, in which de Soto and the expedition encounter the benevolent female ruler of the province of Cofachiqui, he laments that she has not converted to Catholicism (388). Once again, El Inca presents his critique in such a way that de Soto and his men are not entirely responsible for their omission. They have the most noble of intentions but, according to El Inca, are prevented from acting upon them by circumstances beyond their control.

Later in the narrative, El Inca reemphasizes that the failure to settle the land is not because of de Soto's intentions when he states that de Soto had made plans to make a settlement along the banks of the Río Grande (Mississippi River) but was prevented from doing so by circumstances (436). No doubt El Inca is aware that preaching was not on the agenda of de Soto and the opportunists who accompanied him, but he is creating, through his narrative, an ideal type, not a faithful representation of reality.

El Inca sets this tone of exoneration for de Soto's sins of omission early in his narrative. In Book II, Part II, Chapter XVI, he laments the fact that the Spanish did not invite the noble chief Mucozo to be baptized, but he does not indict de Soto and his men for this failure, saying that they had intended to convert the natives after they had made a permanent settlement in the region (229).

On another occasion, El Inca once again touches on the theme of evangelism when relating the episode of Diego de Guzmán, the soldier who abandoned the expedition for the love of an Indian woman. It is interesting that El Inca does not criticize Guzmán for initiating the relationship, but he does criticize him for violating military codes of conduct by deserting the army. It is not surprising that El Inca does not criticize the relationship, given that he is the product of the same type of relationship, although this attitude does seem to conflict with his much-emphasized Catholic zeal. El Inca says he will leave Guzmán's actions for the clergy to judge (433). In this way, he cleverly avoids condemning an act that is the very same type as that in which his parents had engaged. He goes on to suggest that Guzmán could be forgiven entirely if he were to convert to Catholicism the Indians with whom he lives (433–34).

The spirit of evangelistic zeal remains strong from the beginning to the end of El Inca's narrative. Consider, for example, the passage in Book VI, Chapter XX, in which he cites as an example to his countrymen Gonzalo Quadrado Xaramillo, who had been one of the best soldiers of the expedition and who, disgusted and troubled by the violence he had witnessed, entered a religious order along with several other members of the expedition. El Inca notes that, upon arriving in Mexico in 1543, several survivors of the expedition abandon their military careers for religious ones (549–50). El Inca seems to be making the case, once again, for a more peaceful approach to colonization. The members of the expedition who join religious orders realize, based upon their experiences in La Florida, that it might serve everyone concerned much better to preach to the Amerindians instead of fighting them. Had the natives of Mexico and Peru been able to inflict the same kind of damage on the Spanish invaders that the natives of La Florida inflicted upon de Soto and his troops, history would have witnessed an entirely different colonial experience. Unfortunately, as long as the Spanish were winning, the majority did not care about the moral implications of their actions.

El Inca's Prophetic Voice

El Inca is an interpreter of reality, as well as a historian. He interprets what was, what is, and what is possible. He recognizes the implicit imperfection in human nature that causes people to ignore the ideal of that which is possible and to pursue instead the shortsighted objective of short-term gain. He highlights how the attitude of *avoiding a dialogue on the essential questions creates a social structure that justifies and perpetuates erroneous thinking.* He believes that the conflicts between the Spanish and Amerindian cultures are caused by this dialogue avoidance by the Spaniards and that establishing an empathetic dialogue between the two cultures will heal the conflict.

The Spaniards are not interested in a dialogue with the inhabitants of the New World. The Amerindians at times are interested in a dialogue with the Spaniards, but they are stopped by Spanish exploitation. El Inca recognizes that without a realistic dialogue neither European nor Native American can comprehend that the key to a better society and a better future lies in addressing the issues of social injustice and the desire for freedom; that without a dialogue on these issues, the European is limited to a spiritually impoverished existence, obsessed with accumulating wealth and social status; and that this spiritually impoverished state will result in disaster for Native Americans as their culture is dismembered to support the Europeans' obsessions. El Inca is acutely aware that this is the formula that led to the destruction of his mother's Quechua society, and it is what he seeks to preempt in North America.

The Europeans have relegated the Amerindians to a subservient status. Since most of their cultures lack written languages, they have no written history, and they have no voice. El Inca wants to record their history and to give them a way to express their intelligence and spread their wisdom. He sees their noble acts lost to recorded history unless he speaks on their behalf.

To give the natives of La Florida a written history, El Inca combines the oral history about the de Soto expedition given to him by the old soldier, Silvestre, with the oral history that he was taught about his Amerindian heritage. For this reason, he calls his creation *The Florida of the Inca*. His discourse contains parallel narratives: the oral history he is recording and the exposition that all people are one nation. This writing on behalf of the New World population represents a way to overcome European opposition to accepting a dialogue with the New World inhabitants.

Throughout *La Florida*, El Inca calls himself the intermediary who transforms the oral into the written; because he is a mestizo, he is the personification of the link between Amerindian and European. He is geographically and intellectually connected to Imperial Spain, but he is emotionally attached to the indigenous empire of his mother's people. He shows his allegiance to his ancestral heritage by presenting as equals the "heroic gentlemen, Spaniards and Indians," as he boldly asserts in the subtitle of his book.

El Inca is visionary in his evaluations. Through his universalist ideal, he sees the New World natives with equality in the world community upon their conversion to the Catholic faith. He sees their moral and intellectual stature elevated. He sees the conflicts between Native Americans and Europeans overcome by dialogue between the two. He sees Spaniards and Amerindians coexisting in peace in La Florida, each culture enhanced by the other.

El Inca is not to escape the attitudes in the Spanish psyche that create violent acts against the New World natives by conquest participants. As a mestizo in Spain, he experiences marginalization, and the recognition that he craves eludes him as he seeks to become integrated into the Spanish community. He seeks his legitimacy and inclusiveness as he tries to convince Europeans to give legitimacy and inclusiveness to Amerindians.

Throughout his life, El Inca sought to reconcile the Old World and New World cultures in his mestizo heritage. José Durand, the Garcilaso scholar, notes in "El Inca Garcilaso, historiador apasionado" ("El Inca Garcilaso, passionate historian") that El Inca sees himself and the natives of the New World as a dispossessed people: "de un momento a otro El Inca se encontró con que había perdido su hogar, irremediablemente. . . . Alude a la separación de sus padres a causa de nuevas ordenanzas . . . era cosa de su destino más oculto: años después sería también, de manera inexorable, un hombre sin patria" (154) ("from one moment to another El Inca encounters that which he lost. . . . He alludes to the separation of his parents caused by the new laws . . . It was the hardest part of his fate: years later he would be, once again, a man without a country").

A Peruvian expatriate, a mestizo, isolated in his Spanish society, ignored and bored, El Inca begins to write. He begins by translating the Italian in Hebreo's *Dialoghi di amore* into Spanish. In the semiliterate society that exists in Spain in the time in which El Inca is writing, the written word carries a legitimacy that it does not carry today. As he begins to write, he begins to gain the legitimacy and recognition that he has sought so long. With the recognition gained by his writing he hopes to become integrated into his society and end the ambiguity into which his mestizo status has cast him; he hopes and pleads that, through his acceptance, Europeans will extend the same opportunities to natives throughout the New World.

El Inca is encouraged by the success of his translation, and he writes and publishes his second book, *La Florida del Inca.* Through his visionary interpretations of Silvestre's oral account of the de Soto expedition, combined with his Amerindian experiences in Peru, he hopes that the reality of an individual—himself—and a people—Amerindians—seeking freedom from marginalization and a place in the colonization that has occurred and the colonization that is yet to come will be changed by his universalist paradigm into a reality of inclusion. He hopes to place himself and the indigenous peoples of the New World into the historiography of the colonial epoch.

To his Spanish audience, he interprets a less violent and more productive governance in the colonies. He believes that the Spanish explorers should abandon warfare and seek honest work. He condemns, albeit implicitly, the ruthless exploitation the Spaniards practice in the colonies. One can sense El Inca's implicit criticism of the motives behind the conquest when he notes that his inability to accurately describe some of the geographical confines of La Florida is caused, in part, by a careless lack of accurate record keeping by participants in the de Soto expedition. He notes with some contempt that this lack of diligence was caused by their obsessive preoccupation with locating material wealth in their explorations. He knows that the Europeans will remain enslaved in their materialism, justifying and perpetuating their erroneous thinking, unless they accept an appropriate dialogue with the La Florida natives.

According to the norms of sixteenth-century Spanish society, El Inca's informant, Gonzalo Silvestre, is not a marginalized person. By identifying the old soldier as the authority and himself as scribe and interpreter, El Inca can be sure his work escapes his marginalization and receives legitimacy; he is free to shape the *La Florida* narrative in a way that allows him to insert his visions and expressions; he can say things he could not have said had he claimed sole authorship of his narrative; he can give his interpretation of the conflict that is the source of his disillusionment and resentment. The reality that El Inca evokes in *La Florida* is not just the reality presented by his informant, it is the reality of the mestizo experience. His thoughts are transliterated into the thoughts of another, less stigmatized, person and become more acceptable to the European reader. This rhetorical tactic is reinforced by his constant pretense of humility and his apologetic attitude about his self-proclaimed lack of intellectual ability.

With a written version of the de Soto expedition told to him by Gonzalo

Silvestre, El Inca inserts his ideas into the social order in a way that would have been impossible had he written an original text about his ideas. His social ideal, if accepted by society at large, will marginalize marginalization. El Inca takes advantage of lapses in Silvestre's narrative to insert, from his own memory, characteristics of an ethnic group that is very similar to his own. He becomes a participant in shaping the destiny of the natives of La Florida.

His clever attribution of his narrative provides him cover as he implicitly critiques the manner in which the Spanish carry on the colonization process. He wants the reader to believe that any implicit criticism of the Spanish or elevation of the Amerindians is not by design. He demystifies the motives behind the La Florida exploration, pointing out that de Soto and his explorers are obsessed with locating gold, silver, pearls, and other material wealth and that interest in carrying out the king's instructions to convert the natives and to treat them kindly is a pretense only. They commit violent acts against the natives, stealing food from their storehouses and fields, occupying their houses, and enslaving them as guides, interpreters, and burden bearers.

El Inca is a peace advocate. He abhors conflict and violence such as he witnessed in Peru in his youth. He seeks to effect change through language rather than with arms, which is predominantly the way in which relationships between Spaniards and New World natives were shaped previously. Through embracing the *Dialogues* and its Neoplatonic philosophy and through becoming a Catholic lay worker to such an extent that he adopts the monk's habit in later years, he exhibits his peace advocacy.

An intolerance to the boredom created by his idleness caused him to seek escape by reading Hebreo's *Dialoghi di amore* and sparked his interest in its translation. Conflict was the spark that ignited the compulsions and the genius within El Inca that led him to create *La Florida del Inca.* The difference between what Gonzalo Silvestre says and what El Inca writes is where we see the conflict from which his writings originate.

El Inca's writings represent a process of creation of an idealized world to which he longs to see his fellow human beings aspire. *La Florida* is El Inca's first attempt at creating a new discourse. He initiates a new discourse on European-Amerindian relations. He presents his idealized vision of the relationship between Amerindians and Europeans, and in the process, he creates a sense of identity for himself—writer/scribe and mestizo.

La Florida del Inca is a compilation of history, literature, philosophy, sociopolitical propaganda, and autobiography. Its esthetic qualities place it among the great literary works of sixteenth-century Spain. Its poetic qualities remind one of Ercilla's *La Araucana,* and its sympathetic representation of Native Americans is reminiscent of the works of the great defender of indigenous rights, Bartolomé de las Casas. All three seek to elevate the native civilizations of the Americas and to show that they are, in many respects, not only equal to but also very similar to Hispanic civilization.

The book is also an allegory of the misguided nature of the Spanish enterprise in the New World. Through the tragic figure of de Soto, El Inca personifies society's error in a way that makes *La Florida* more than just a history; he raises his narrative to the allegorical level. The allegory is created by El Inca through his mastery of writing—the predominant European rhetorical device—using an interpretive approach that creates the desired reaction on the part of the reader and brings into sharp focus the reality of colonialism.

In *La Florida,* we see the successful implementation of the Renaissance tool of the "eyewitness account" to refute popular beliefs about the colonial experience (Zamora 39). As Zamora points out, this type of chronicle had a profound effect on popular discourse because it challenged the version of history written by the king's official historians:

> One can, in fact, divide Colonial Latin American historical narrative into two general types: the bookish histories written from a distance and lacking direct contact with the material, and those which challenged them based on the authority of eyewitness testimony, either as an attribute of the actual narrator of the account or of the privileged source on whose prerogative the validity of the history rests. (40)

El Inca writes with a specific purpose and thus embellishes the historical narrative with his own ideology. From the perspective of a literary scholar, "all historical writing is ideologically marked, and insofar as historical texts present a certain view of the historical record, they employ a series of narrative tactics of emplotment and argumentation in order to render that record intelligible to the intended audience" (Zamora 4).

El Inca's work represents a break with a popular rhetoric that will not acknowledge indigenous rights. El Inca denounces, largely by implicit means, a discourse that ignores the value of the human being and reestablishes the reality that all the people of the earth, in any given era, in any given locality, belong to the same human race and are entitled to equal consideration with respect to their rights as human beings.

With his first original work, El Inca gives us a book that is visionary and somewhat prophetic. Its message is better understood centuries after its creation. El Inca's *mestizaje* and his vision of the global blending of ethnic groups and cultures accurately predict the future of humanity. He predicts the concept of the global village before the global village becomes a reality. The concept of the universal being relates to the prophetic words of El Inca.

Over centuries, exploitation and abuse received preeminence upon the world stage. Only recently, once again, have universal equality and brotherhood received recognition through the indigenous rights movements of North, Central, and South America.

La Florida del Inca is everything its author intends, as a result of its author's mastery of his craft and his enlightened approach to his subject. El Inca represents the best of the writers of the Golden Age of Spanish letters who, as the great Golden Age poet Luis de Góngora observes, are renowned "tanto por plumas cuanto por espadas" (390) ("as much for their pens as for their swords"). Literary excellence and historical analysis stand out in El Inca's writings each time they are studied anew.

La Florida is as relevant today as it was in 1605. It will remain so because the ideals of El Inca Garcilaso de la Vega transcend time and space.

Works Cited

Asensio, Eugenio. "Dos cartas desconocidas del Inca Garcilaso." *Nueva Revista de Filología Hispánica* 1953(7):583–89.

Avalle-Arce, Juan Bautista. *Antología Vívida*. Madrid: Editorial Gredos, 1964.

Bancroft, George. *History of the United States: From the Discovery of the American Continent*. Boston: Littlebrown, 1837.

Biedma, Luys Hernández. *Relation of the Island of Florida*. Trans. John E. Worth. In *The De Soto Chronicles*, vol. 1. Eds. Lawrence A. Clayton, Vernon James Knight, Jr., and Edward C. Moore. Pp. 221–46. Tuscaloosa: University of Alabama Press, 1993.

Brading, D. A. *The First America: The Spanish Monarchy, Creole Patriots and the Liberal State 1492–1867*. Cambridge: Cambridge University Press, 1991.

Cabeza de Vaca, Alvar Núñez. *Naufragios*. Ed. Juan Francisco Maura. Madrid: Ediciones Cátedra, 1996.

Calderón, Ventura García. Introducción. In *Comentarios reales: páginas escogidas. El Inca Garcilaso de la Vega*. Ed. Ventura Garcia Calderón. Paris: Desclés deBrouwer, 1938.

Castanien, Donald G. *El Inca Garcilaso de la Vega*. New York: Twayne, 1969.

Clayton, Lawrence A. Foreword. In *The De Soto Chronicles*, vol. 1. Eds. Lawrence A. Clayton, Vernon James Knight, Jr., and Edward C. Moore. Pp. xix–xx. Tuscaloosa: University of Alabama Press, 1993.

Crowley, Frances G. "Garcilaso de la Vega, the Inca." In *The De Soto Chronicles*, vol. 2. Eds. Lawrence A. Clayton, Vernon James Knight, Jr., and Edward C. Moore. Pp. 1–24. Tuscaloosa: University of Alabama Press, 1993.

Dowling, Lee. "La Florida del Inca: Garcilaso's Literary Sources." In *The Hernando de Soto Expedition: History, Historiography, and Discovery in the Southeast*. Ed. Patricia Galloway. Pp. 98–154. Lincoln: University of Nebraska Press, 1997.

Durand, José. "El Inca Garcilaso, historiador apasionado." *Cuadernos Americanos* 1950(4):153–58.

Elvas, Fidalgo de. *True Relation of the Hardships Suffered by Gov. Don Hernando de Soto and Certain Portuguese Gentlemen in the Discovery of Florida*. Trans. James A. Robertson. In *The De Soto Chronicles*, vol. 2. Eds. Lawrence A. Clayton, Vernon James Knight, Jr., and Edward C. Moore. Pp. 19–219. Tuscaloosa: University of Alabama Press, 1993.

Ercilla, Alonso de. *La Araucana*. Ed. Ofelia Garza del Castillo. México City: Editorial Porrua, 1968.

Galloway, Patricia. "The Incestuous Soto Narratives." In *The Hernando de Soto Expedition: History, Historiography, and Discovery in the Southeast*. Ed. Patricia Galloway. Pp. 11–44. Lincoln: University of Nebraska Press, 1997.

Garcilaso de la Vega, El Inca. *Comentarios reales de los Incas*. In *Obras completas del Inca Garcilazo de la Vega*, vol. 2. Ed. Carmelo Saenz de Santa María. Madrid: Ediciones Atlas, 1960.

———. *Diálogos del amor*. In *Obras completas del Inca Garcilazo de la Vega*, vol. 1. Ed. Carmelo Saenz de Santa María. Madrid: Ediciones Atlas, 1960.

———. *La Florida del Inca*. In *Obras completas del Inca Garcilazo de la Vega*, vol. 1. Ed. Carmelo Saenz de Santa María. Madrid: Ediciones Atlas, 1960.

———. *The Florida of the Inca*. Trans. John G. Varner and Jeannette Varner. Austin: University of Texas Press, 1962.

———. *La Florida del Inca*. Ed. Sylvia-Lynn Hilton. Alcalá: Fundación Universitaria Española, 1982.

———. *La Florida by the Inca*. Trans. Charmion Shelby. In *The De Soto Chronicles*, vol. 2. Eds. Lawrence A. Clayton, Vernon James Knight, Jr., and Edward C. Moore. Pp. 25–559. Tuscaloosa: University of Alabama Press, 1993.

———. *Genealogy of Garcí Pérez de Vargas*. Trans. Frances G. Crowley. In *The De Soto Chronicles*, vol. 2. Eds. Lawrence A. Clayton, Vernon James Knight, Jr., and Edward C. Moore. Pp. 563–76. Tuscaloosa: University of Alabama Press, 1993.

———. *Historia general del Perú*. In *Obras completas del Inca Garcilazo de la Vega*, vol. 3. Ed. Carmelo Saenz de Santa María. Madrid: Ediciones Atlas, 1960.

———. *Relación de la descendencia de Garcí Pérez de Vargas*. In *Obras completas del Inca Garcilazo de la Vega*, vol. 1. Ed. Carmelo Saenz de Santa María. Pp. 229–40. Madrid: Ediciones Atlas, 1960.

Góngora, Luis de. *Obras completas*. Eds. Juan Mille y Giménez and Isabel Mille y Giménez. 1 vol. Madrid: Aguilar, 1943.

Henige, David. "So Unbelievable It Has to Be True: Inca Garcilaso in Two Worlds." In *The Hernando de Soto Expedition: History, Historiography, and Discovery in the Southeast*. Ed. Patricia Galloway. Pp. 155–80. Lincoln: University of Nebraska Press, 1997.

Hernández, Max. "A Childhood Memory: Time, Place, and Subjective Experience." *Modern Language Notes* 1990:317–30.

Hoffman, Paul E. "Introduction: The De Soto Expedition, A Cultural Crossroads." In *The De Soto Chronicles*, vol. 1. Eds. Lawrence A. Clayton, Vernon James Knight, Jr., and Edward C. Moore. Pp. 1–17. Tuscaloosa: University of Alabama Press, 1993.

Hudson, Charles M. *The Juan Pardo Expeditions and Exploration of the Carolinas and Tennessee 1566–1568*. Washington, D.C.: Smithsonian Institution Press, 1990.

Janiga-Perkins, Constance. *Immaterial Transcendences: Colonial Subjectivity as Process in Brazil's Letter of Discovery (1500)*. New York: Peter Lang, 2001.

Lapesa, Rafael. *Introducción a los estudios literarios*. Madrid: Ediciones Cátedra, 1981.

Las Casas, Bartolomé de. *Brevísima relación de la destrucción de las Indias*. Ed. Manuel B. Gaiabrios. Madrid: Fundación Universitaria Española, 1977.

Leonard, Irving A. *Books of the Brave*. New York: Gordian, 1964.

———. "The Inca Garcilaso de la Vega, First Classic Writer of America." In *Filología y Crítica Hispánica: Homenaje al Profesor Frederico Sánchez Escribano*. Eds. Alberto Porqueras Mayo and Carlos Rojas. Pp. 51–62. Madrid: Ediciones Alcalá, 1969.

Lockhart, James. *The Men of Cajamarca: A Social and Biographical Study of the First Conquerors of Peru*. Austin: University of Texas Press, 1972.

MacLeod, Murdo J. "Aspects of the Internal Economy of Colonial Spanish America: Labour, Taxation, Distribution and Exchange." In *The Cambridge History of Latin American*, vol. 2. Ed. Leslie Bethell. Pp. 341–88. Cambridge: Cambridge University Press, 1984.

Mazzotti, José Antonio. "The Lightening Bolt Yields to the Rainbow: Indigenous History and Colonial Semiosis in the *Royal Commentaries* of El Inca Garcilaso de la Vega." *A Journal of Literary History* 1996(57):197–211.

Menéndez y Pelayo, Marcelino. *Historia de la poesía hispano-americana*, vol. 2. Ed. Enrique Sánchez Reyes. Pp. 76–77. Madrid: Santander, 1948.

Ortega, Julio. "The Discourse of Abundance." *Review of Latin American Art and Literature* 1990(43):3–7.

Oviedo, Gonzalo F. *Historia general y natural de las Indias*. Ed. Juan Pérez Buesco. Madrid: Ediciones Atlas, 1950.

Pastor, Beatriz. *Discursos narrativos de la Conquista: mitificación y emergencia*. Hanover: Ediciones del Norte, 1988.

Pratt, Mary Louise. "Apocalipsis en los Andes." *Américas* 1999(August):38–47.

Prescott, William H. *History of the Conquest of Peru*. 2 vols. New York: Kelnscott Society, 1847.

Pupo-Walker, Enrique. *Historia, creación y profecía en los textos del Inca Garcilaso de la Vega*. Madrid: José Porrúa Turanzas, 1982.

Quesada, Aurelio Miró. *El Inca Garcilaso y otros estudios garcilasistas*. Madrid: Ediciones Cultura Hispánica, 1971.

Rabasa, José. *Inventing America: Spanish Historiography and the Formation of Eurocentrism*. Norman: University of Oklahoma Press, 1993.

Rangel, Rodrigo. *Account of the Northern Conquest and Discovery of Hernando de Soto*. Trans. John E. Worth. In *The De Soto Chronicles*, vol. 1. Eds. Lawrence A. Clayton, Vernon James Knight, Jr., and Edward C. Moore. Pp. 247–306. Tuscaloosa: University of Alabama Press, 1993.

Robertson, James A. Preface. In *The De Soto Chronicles*, vol. 1. Eds. Lawrence A. Clayton, Vernon James Knight, Jr., and Edward C. Moore. Pp. 23–27. Tuscaloosa: University of Alabama Press, 1993.

Ross, Kathleen. "Historians of the Conquest and Colonization of the New World: 1550–1620." In *The Cambridge History of Latin American Literature*, vol. 1. Eds. Roberto González Echevarría and Enrique Pupo-Walker. Pp. 101–42. Cambridge: Cambridge University Press, 1996.

Schwartz, Robert N. *Peru: Country in Search of a Nation*. Los Angeles: Inter-American, 1970.

Smith, Marvin T. "Indian Responses to European Contact: The Coosa Example." In *First Encounters: Spanish Explorations in the Caribbean and the United States, 1492–1570*. Eds. Jerald T. Milanich and Susan Milbrath. Pp. 135–49. Gainesville: University Press of Florida, 1989.

Varner, John G. *El Inca: The Life and Times of Garcilaso de la Vega.* Austin: University of Texas Press, 1968.

Wise, Terence, and Angus McBride. *The Conquistadores.* Oxford: Osprey, 1999.

Zamora, Margarita. *Language, Authority, and Indigenous History in the Comentarios Reales de los Incas.* Cambridge: Cambridge University Press, 1988.

Index

status of, 9–10; and El Inca's inheritance, 8, 15–16, 18; friendship with Silvestre, 40; role in Peruvian civil war, 7, 8–9

Gasca, Pedro de la, 8, 9, 27

Girón, Francisco Hernández, 27

Gold, 50, 51–52. *See also* Wealth

Góngora, Luis de, 116

Guerrilla warfare, 83, 87, 88

Guzmán, Diego de, 109

Guzmán, Fernán Pérez de, 9

Harquebus, 86–87

Hebreo, León el, 19, 22, 108. *See also Dialoghi di amore*

Henige, David, 43, 56, 57, 59

Hernández, Max, 45, 59

Herrera de Alcántara, Spain, 39

Hidalgos, 9, 15

Hirrihigua, 71, 91

Historia general del Perú, 13, 26–27, 98

Hoffman, Paul, 100

House of Pedro Crasbeeck, 24

Hualipa, 3

Huallpa Tupac Inca Yupanqui, 10

Huarina, Battle of, 8

Huáscar, 2, 3, 4, 10

Huayna Capac, 1–2, 3, 10, 25

Hudson, Charles, 86

Idealization, by El Inca: of de Soto, 99, 100, 101, 105, 109; of the de Soto expedition, 99, 101, 102, 105, 106, 107, 108; of the land and people of La Florida, 58, 59, 93; of Native Americans, 66–67, 90, 93; of the relationship between Native Americans and Europeans, 114

Incas: conquest of Peru, 1–5; culture of, 63; custom of eliminating the negative from history, 24, 46, 59; oral history of, 1–2, 3, 9, 10; oral history of in El Inca's education, 11, 13

Index of prohibited books, 22, 90. *See also* Inquisition Committee

Indian mounds, 77–79

Inquisition Committee, 22, 65, 71, 90

Janiga-Perkins, Constance, 54

Jesuits, 20

Knight, Vernon James, Jr., viiin2, 79

La Araucana, 67, 68, 69, 70–72, 101, 114. *See also* Ercilla, Alonso de

La Florida: description of territory, 34–35; El Inca's descriptions of the land, 47–54; naming of, 33; Spanish exploration of, 32–36

Lapesa, Rafael, 27–28, 47

Las Casas, Bartolomé de, 64, 65, 66; as advocate for the Native Americans, 7n7, 114; depiction of the Indians, 68–69; and The New Laws, 6

Las Posadas, 39

Leonard, Irving A., 69, 95, 103, 104

Lima. *See* Los Reyes

Literary styles that influenced El Inca, 38n16, 46, 70. *See also* Classical antiquity, literary style and paradigms of; Epic style, influence of on *La Florida*; Romances, chivalric

López, Juan, 106, 107

Los Reyes, 7, 8, 14

McBride, Angus, 84, 87, 88

Manco Capac, 2n3, 25

Martel de los Ríos, Luisa, 12

Marten skins, 52, 53

Maura, Juan Francisco, 50

Mauvilla, 84, 90, 97

Mayta Capac, 25

Mazzotti, Jose Antonio, 44

Mendoza, Andrés Hurtado de, 27

Menéndez y Pelayo, Marcelino, 25

Mestizos: definition, viiin1, 1; status in Peru, 13, 24; status in Spain, 15, 24, 108. *See also under* Garcilaso de la Vega, El Inca

Mexía, Agustín, 23

Mexía, Pedro, 20, 104

Mississippian culture, 77–79

Mococo, 58–59

Montesa, Carlos, 22

Montilla, Spain, 15, 17–18, 20, 30, 107

Moore, Edward C., viiin2

Morales, Ambrosio de, 21

More, Sir Thomas, *Utopia*, 46

Morisco rebellion, 18, 64, 86

Moscoso, Luis de, 106

Mucozo, 109